Mary Ford
Oxford
June 2000.

Expressing the Sacred

An Introduction to the Phenomenology of Religion

James L. Cox

First edition 1992

Published by
University of Zimbabwe Publications
P.O. Box MP 203
Mount Pleasant
Harare
Zimbabwe

ISBN 0–908307–28–4

Cover photograph by the author of the Imbahura Mountain, Mberengwa, Zimbabwe, under care of the Chingoma Spirit

Phototypeset by University of Zimbabwe Publications
Printed by Mazongororo Paper Converters (Pvt.) Ltd., Harare

To the late

Revd Collen Zhuwawo

BA (Hons.), 1991

Contents

List of tables and figures

Preface

Religion is a human phenomenon. Nothing religious, therefore, ultimately can be alien to the human experience. Religion, moreover, forms one component among others comprising the whole of human activity and understanding. The study of this component forms a discipline in its own right and should not be subsumed under other academic studies within the human sciences.

Since religion forms its own subject matter, a methodology for its study is required. Throughout this century, scholars of religion have developed such methods, for example, those of comparative religion, the history of religion or religions and the phenomenology of religion. These methods may be categorized as *the general science of religion*, the German *Allgemeine Religionswissenschaft* (see Fig. 3.1).

This book endeavours to explore the phenomenology of religion in a way which incorporates *Allgemeine Religionswissenschaft*. This means that the phenomenology of religion is interpreted to include what has been called the comparative study of religion and the history of religions. As the phenomenology of religion is described in the following pages, a particular methodology is adopted which aims at descriptions and at explanations so as to produce an understanding of religion itself.

This book is intended as an introduction to the study of religious methodology. Part I outlines the method and Part II focuses on the phenomena themselves. The first-year student may wish to stop at the end of Part II as Part III is more advanced and includes some finer distinctions which are of interest to those intending to specialize further in religious studies and particularly in methodological approaches to the study of religion. Part III, which aims at achieving an understanding of the meaning of religion, may, therefore, be used quite profitably by students who have studied Parts I and II previously in an introductory course.

In addition this book is intended to fill a gap in texts used in introductory courses to religion. Some books concentrate on discussing religion itself, including aspects of the phenomena such as myths and rituals, and tend to move very quickly over the methodology and pay only minimal attention to the phenomenological approach. Other books describe the religions of the world, but again spend little time on methods for attaining such descriptions.

One final point should be noted at the outset. Many authors have tended to dissociate the phenomenology of religion from the philosophical movement which bears the same name. I believe, however, that philosophical phenomenology as a method for knowing can be related directly to the method for understanding religious phenomena. This assumption underlies the position of this book: that the phenomenology of religion includes more than descriptions and classifications of various religious activities, but also involves interpretations based on historical and cultural contexts out of which a broad understanding both of specific religions and of religion in general may be attained.

Note to the Second Edition

The second edition of this book remains very much as it appeared originally, since the aim of providing an introductory and user friendly text on the phenomenology of religion remains unchanged. I have added a section in Chapter One on some key philosophical terms used by Husserl which I believe will assist the student in understanding my explanation of his method. I have also added a number of references, mostly secondary, to which the student may wish to refer for a more detailed discussion of philosophical phenomenology. These additional references will direct the student into the primary sources of the philosophers mentioned, if a full and in-depth enquiry into their arguments is desired. The sources I have added, however, are intended to help students who want to understand the basic approach of philosophical phenomenology in greater detail than I am able to provide within the objectives of this book.

I have added at the beginning of Chapter Two an explanation of my step-by-step presentation of the stages in the phenomenology of religion for purposes of clarification. In Chapter Three, I have introduced the student to the current debate over 'reductionism' and the traditional claim of phenomenologists and historians of religion that their subject matter is irreducible to the subject matter of any other discipline. Again, I have not examined here the rather technical nature of this controversy, but the references cited, including my own contribution to the discussions, will direct the student toward the relevant sources if further studies in this area are of interest.

Finally, I have endeavoured to correct any errors, either factual or typographical, which may have appeared in the first edition.

Acknowledgements

I would like to express my gratitude first of all to the students in the Department of Religious Studies, Classics and Philosophy at the University of Zimbabwe who discussed the subjects contained in this book with me in tutorials and in small discussion groups. They posed significant questions, raised important issues and challenged (helpfully) many of the assumptions of this book. This interaction has produced a number of revisions both in style and content. A special dedication is offered to the late Revd Collen

Zhuwawo, whose BA Honours thesis forms the case study for the method in Chapter Four.

I would also like to thank Dr E. C. Mandivenga, formerly Chairman of the same Department, and Professor M. F. C. Bourdillon of the Sociology Department, University of Zimbabwe, and Dr G. Muzorewa formerly of the United Theological College in Harare for reviewing the text and offering helpful comments. Meaningful discussions have been held with Professor F. Verstraelen of the University of Zimbabwe whose expertise in the history of Christianity in Africa has assisted me in clarifying some points on why the phenomenology of religion developed. I also owe much to the influence of two of my mentors, Professor Andrew Walls, Director of the Centre for the Study of Christianity in the non-Western World in Edinburgh, and Professor Harold Turner, from whom I learned more than I realized at the time while doing my doctoral studies at the University of Aberdeen.

I also wish to express my gratitude to the Publications Committee of the University of Zimbabwe for agreeing to publish this text in its first and second editions, and to Roger Stringer and Caroline MacNaughtan formerly of the Publications Office for their invaluable assistance in editing the manuscript and improving the diagrams. Mr. Samuel Matsangaise, current head of University Publications, has been most helpful in the preparation of the second edition. I want to express my thanks to him and his staff for their efficient handling and distribution of this version of the book.

James L. Cox
Harare
Edinburgh
1995

PART I

The Phenomenology of Religion

Chapter One
Religion and Phenomenology

The subject of this book is the 'phenomenology of religion'. Before we can discuss this subject, we must address two preliminary questions: What is religion? and What is phenomenology? We will then be in a position to explore the phenomenology of religion as a whole.

We begin by looking at definitions of religion in order to gain a general understanding of our field of study. What can we include or exclude as religious phenomena? In the process of answering this, however, we discover that obtaining definitions prior to engaging in the study of religion can be a sterile academic exercise. Our later discussions of the phenomenological method endeavour to resolve this central problem in defining the meaning of religion.

Another reason for beginning with definitions is to demonstrate how complicated the field of religion is and why naïve assumptions about human religious experience need to be challenged and deepened. As we analyse the definitions in this chapter, this complexity should become apparent.

Despite the problems encountered in defining religion, we need to develop some basic guidelines at the outset on which to base our later analyses. If we do not do this, we may fall into the logical inconsistency of proposing to study something which we claim cannot be defined prior to studying it! How then will we know *what* to study? In order to overcome this dilemma, I opt later in this chapter for a flexible 'working' definition rather than proposing a prescriptive statement of what religion is or is not.

What is religion?

Scholars from different disciplines have been interested in the field of religion. In his book on the religions of the world, John Ferguson (1978, 13–17) lists seventeen definitions which can be organized into the following categories: theological, moral, philosophical, psychological and sociological. Following a brief description of Ferguson's examples, there is a summary statement listing the central criterion for each type of definition. (For a summary of Ferguson's definitions, see Table 1.1.)

Theological definitions of religion

Definitions which insist that religion has to do with God or supernatural

Table 1.1

SUMMARY OF FERGUSON'S DEFINITIONS OF RELIGION

Theological definitions
a) Religion is believing in God.
b) Religion is belief in spiritual beings.
c) Religion is the life of God in the soul of man.
d) Religion is a mystery, at once awesome and attractive.

Moral definitions
a) Religion is leading a good life.
b) Religion is morality tinged with emotion.
c) Religion is the recognition of all our duties as divine commands.
d) Religion is a sum of scruples which impede the free use of our faculties.

Philosophical definitions
a) Religion is what a man does with his solitariness.
b) Religion is the relation of man to his own being, but as a being outside of himself.
c) Religion is ultimate concern.

Psychological definitions
a) Religion is the result of seeking comfort in a world which, dispassionately considered, is a terrifying wilderness.
b) Religion is some kind of profound inner experience.
c) Religion is a universal obsessive neurosis.

Sociological definitions
a) Religion is the opium of the people.
b) Religion is the conservation of values.
c) Religion is a co-operative quest after a completely satisfying life.

Source: Ferguson (1978).

spiritual powers of some sort may be termed theological definitions of religion. Ferguson's examples of this type are as follows:
a) 'Religion is believing in God.' This definition is credited by Ferguson to a schoolboy who offers a common-sense approach to the question, 'What is religion?' The thirteenth-century theologian, St. Thomas Aquinas (1225–74), said something quite similar when he announced that 'religion denotes properly a relation to God' (cited by Hall, Pilgrim and Cavanagh, 1986, 6).

b) 'Religion is belief in spiritual beings.' This is a rough summary of the view of the nineteenth-century anthropologist, E. B. Tylor. We will discuss Tylor in detail later, but it is enough to note here that he held that, in its earliest form, religion involved a belief in a hierarchy of spirits from the lower to the most powerful beings.

c) 'Religion is the life of God in the soul of man.' This comes from the nineteenth-century theologian, W. Newton Clarke. It stresses the two realities of God and the soul, belief in both of which are necessary for religion to exist.

d) 'Religion is a mystery, at once awesome and attractive.' This statement is derived from the twentieth-century German philosopher, Rudolph Otto, who found the 'essence of religion' in the idea of the holy which he claimed attracts people owing to its mystery and its power. Although this need not be regarded as a theological definition in the sense of asserting the existence of a 'holy being', it can be classified under this heading since it defines religion in terms of a spiritual realm outside of the human (that is, in terms of 'God', 'spirits', 'an awesome mystery').

The four examples above help us summarize the theological definitions of religion as follows:

A theological definition makes the central criterion of religion belief in a transcendent power which is usually personified as a Supreme Being, but is sometimes conceived as being diffused through powerful spiritual beings, or is held to be an impersonal, mysterious, supernatural force.

Moral definitions of religion

Definitions which stress that religion consists of telling its adherents how they ought to live may be termed moral definitions. Examples of this type are:

a) 'Religion is leading a good life.' This is another common-sense definition and is attributed by Ferguson to a schoolgirl. It simply asserts that to be religious is to be moral without defining what morality entails.

b) 'Religion is morality tinged with emotion.' This comes from the nineteenth-century British writer Matthew Arnold. It complements the schoolgirl's common-sense answer by insisting that human emotions or feelings must accompany the moral understanding for religion to be present.

c) 'Religion is the recognition of all our duties as divine commands.' This is a form of the eighteenth-century philosopher Immanuel Kant's 'categorical imperative', which contends that there is a moral law which we all 'ought' to obey. Religion exists when that moral law is interpreted as a commandment from God.

d) 'Religion is a sum of scruples which impede the free use of our faculties.' Ferguson attributes this definition to Salomon Reinach, an early twentieth-century historian of religions. Although it implies a negative reaction towards religion, it identifies the function of religion as the enforcing of external laws, attitudes or customs by divine decree and thus can be classified as a moral definition.

The above examples can be summarized as follows:

A moral definition makes the central criterion of religion a code of correct behaviour generally affirmed by believers as having its source in an unquestioned and unquestionable authority.

Philosophical definitions

Although related to theological definitions, philosophical definitions generally describe religion in terms of an abstract, usually impersonal, concept. Ferguson cites a number of examples which can be placed within this category.

a) 'Religion is what a man does with his solitariness.' This definition, from the twentieth-century philosopher, Alfred North Whitehead, identifies the abstract notion of solitariness as the fundamental religious dimension within human existence. Presumably, when one achieves a condition or awareness of the solitary (as opposed simply to being alone or lonely), one has achieved a religious experience.

b) 'Religion is the relation of man to his own being, but as a being outside himself.' This assertion is related to the nineteenth-century philosopher Ludwig Feuerbach's theory of religion as a human projection. It defines religion as existing wherever human characteristics (such as love, power, hope, knowledge) are transferred to an imaginary being conceived as being outside, yet perfecting, those human characteristics.

c) 'Religion is ultimate concern.' This famous definition offered by the twentieth-century theologian, Paul Tillich, forms one of the most simple yet basic definitions of religion. For Tillich, religion is a relationship which people hold with that which concerns them ultimately. Obviously, this could be God or spiritual beings, but since it is much broader than this it conveys an abstract idea which can be embodied in a variety of specific objects, symbols or concepts.

The three examples cited above lead to the following summary:

A philosophical definition makes the central criterion for religion the positing of an idea or concept which the believer interprets as ultimate or final in relation to the cosmic order and to human existence.

Psychological definitions

Psychological definitions of religion stress that religion has to do with the emotions, feelings or psychological states of the human in relation to the religious object. Some examples from Ferguson are as follows:

a) 'Religion is the result of seeking comfort in a world which, dispassionately considered, is a terrifying wilderness.' This definition was developed by the twentieth-century philosopher, Bertrand Russell. It stresses that, because of the misfortunes and sufferings they experience in the world, people seek comfort or consolation in religion. As we will see in our later discussion of Sigmund Freud, comfort and consolation are psychological needs.

b) 'Religion is some kind of profound inner experience.' Ferguson attributes this definition to another schoolgirl. Since it stresses inner experience, it can be classified as a psychological definition similar to that offered by the nineteenth-century theologian, Friedrich Schleiermacher, who described religion as 'a feeling of absolute dependence' (quoted by Hall, Pilgrim and Cavanagh, 1986, 5).

c) 'Religion is a universal obsessive neurosis.' This definition falls within the viewpoint of the followers of the psychoanalytic school of Sigmund Freud. It defines religion as a psychological disturbance, one which, although universal, must be overcome if humanity is to attain psychological health.

A summary of psychological definitions is shown below:

A psychological definition makes the central criterion of religion feelings or emotions within people which cause them to appeal to forces greater than themselves to satisfy those feelings.

Sociological definitions

Definitions of religion which emphasize religion as a group consciousness embodying cultural norms or as a product of society in general may be termed sociological definitions. Ferguson's list includes the following which fall within this category:

a) 'Religion is the opium of the people.' This classical definition constructed by Karl Marx indicates that religion results from the oppression of the masses by those in positions of social or economic power who use the message of religion to keep the oppressed content with their lot in this life in the hope of a just order in the next one. Religion thus plays a sociological function for both the oppressor and the oppressed.

b) 'Religion is the conservation of values.' This definition is attributed by

Ferguson to the late nineteenth-/early twentieth-century German philosopher, Harald Höffding, but it reflects a widely held view of traditional sociologists such as Emile Durkheim or the twentieth-century anthropologist, Bronislaw Malinowski. Religion, in this view, is described as a conservative force within society which defines the fundamental values of the group and then maintains and enforces those values by an appeal to supernatural powers.

c) 'Religion is a co-operative quest after a completely satisfying life.' Although this could be viewed as a psychological definition, its emphasis on the co-operative quest places it within the sociological category. Ferguson does not cite a precise source for this quotation, but it sounds quite similar, as we will see later, to the definition offered by the contemporary scholar, Martin Prozesky (1984, 153), that religion is 'a quest for ultimate well-being'. We would conclude from this definition that whenever societies seek to attain the most satisfying life for their members they are exhibiting religious concerns. This is echoed also by the anthropologists, William Lessa and Evon Vogt (1965, 1), who define religion as 'a system of beliefs and practices directed toward the "ultimate concern" of a society'.

The above examples lead to the following summary:

A sociological definition makes the central criterion of religion the existence of a community of people which is identified, bound together and maintained by its beliefs in powers or forces greater than the community itself.

Problems in defining religion

Few of the seventeen definitions of religion cited by Ferguson can be placed neatly into just one of the five categories described above. Some could be put into more than one, such as Rudolph Otto's 'awesome mystery' (theological or philosophical) or Ludwig Feuerbach's perfected human characteristics (philosophical or psychological). But the difficulty in classifying the definitions neatly is just a minor problem.

The diversity of definitions and the lack of agreement on the subject by scholars leaves us with the much more significant problem that *no universal definition of religion exists.* Some modern writers have sought to overcome this problem, firstly by citing the limitations of traditional definitions (such as those listed by Ferguson and summarized in our classifications) and then by offering their own alternatives aimed at overcoming these limitations. We will look at two analyses which have clearly delineated the problems with defining religion and then I will suggest a working definition which seeks to overcome these difficulties.

In their introductory textbook on religion the American scholars Hall, Pilgrim and Cavanagh (1986, 9–10) identify four characteristic problems with traditional definitions of religion; these are: vagueness, narrowness, compartmentalization and prejudice.

Vagueness. Hall, Pilgrim and Cavanagh argue that many definitions are so unclear that they do not distinguish the subject matter of religion from other fields of study. Tillich's definition of religion as 'ultimate concern' or the schoolgirl's statement that religion means 'living a good life' might be accused of this fault.

Narrowness. Some definitions overcompensate for the problem of vagueness by restricting the subject matter of religion and thus exclude too much from the field of study. Hall, Pilgrim and Cavanagh contend, for example, that St. Thomas Aquinas' claim that religion denotes a relationship with God (or the simple idea that religion is a belief in God) narrowly excludes non-theistic or polytheistic forms of religion.

Compartmentalization. Hall, Pilgrim and Cavanagh argue that any definition which explains religion in terms of just one 'single, special aspect' of human life is guilty of compartmentalization; this means reducing religion to one part of life and ignoring its relevance to the totality of human existence. Schleiermacher's definition of religion as a feeling of absolute dependence might do this by reducing religion to a mere psychological condition. Whitehead's definition might also compartmentalize religion by restricting it to the experience of solitariness.

Prejudice. A definition which evaluates in the process of defining cannot present an objective picture of what religion actually is. Several examples of prejudicial definitions are found in Ferguson's list. Marx's argument that religion is the opium of the people is clearly biased. So, too, are Reinach's claim that religion impedes 'the free use of our faculties' and the Freudian contention that religion is a 'universal obsessive neurosis'.

Another approach to the problem of defining religion is found in J. E. Barnhart's *The Study of Religion and its Meaning* (1977, 2–5). Barnhart, like Hall, Pilgrim and Cavanagh, criticizes traditional definitions of religion. Barnhart identifies five issues: belief in the supernatural, evaluative definitions, diluted definitions, expanded definitions and true religion.

Belief in the supernatural. Barnhart denies that religions must hold a belief in God or supernatural beings to qualify as religions. He believes that such definitions restrict the subject matter of religion and thus are too *exclusive.* This then corresponds to what Hall, Pilgrim and Cavanagh call *narrowness.* Barnhart, therefore, considers definitions such as E. B. Tylor's 'religion consists of beliefs in spiritual beings' as being too narrow.

Evaluative definitions. Barnhart agrees with Hall, Pilgrim and Cavanagh that definitions fail if they are prejudiced; and, in common with Hall, Pilgrim and Cavanagh, he cites Marx and Freud as classical examples of this fault. He also adds Tillich to this category since he believes that the idea of ultimate concern is itself an evaluative concept imposed on religion from the perspective of Western philosophy.

Diluted definitions. This type of definition would correspond to what Hall, Pilgrim and Cavanagh call *vagueness.* Barnhart calls this 'the lowest common denominator' definition which is so broad as to include almost everything in the field of religion. Clarke's statement that 'religion is the life of God in the soul of man', actually tells us nothing about either God or the soul and thus suffers, among other faults, from diluting the definition.

Expanded definitions. These are what Hall, Pilgrim and Cavanagh refer to under the term *compartmentalization.* The properties of what define religion are so expanded as to exclude all other aspects of human life. For example, when Bertrand Russell defined religion he expanded its definition so far as to make it seem only an effort to seek comfort in a terrifying world. This reduces religion to a search for consolation and thus compartmentalizes it. If the definition of religion expands the list of what comprises religion so far as to place it within one compartment of human existence, it has the opposite effect of diluting the definition.

True religion. This is the problem of defining all religions in terms of one religion which the definition itself claims to be true. 'Religion is belief in Jesus' or 'There is no God but Allah and Muhammad is his prophet' provide two examples of this. Hall, Pilgrim and Cavanagh would call these definitions prejudiced, but Barnhart's additional category clarifies that prejudice need not result just from an evaluation *against* religion (such as Freud's) but also may include claims of truth or revelation from *within* a religion itself.

Barnhart and Hall, Pilgrim and Cavanagh agree, therefore, on the general problems facing the traditional definitions of religion; Table 1.2 summarizes these problems.

Table 1.2

PROBLEMS WITH DEFINING RELIGION

Hall, Pilgrim and Cavanagh (1986)	*Barnhart (1977)*
vagueness	diluted definitions
narrowness	belief in supernatural
compartmentalization	expanded definitions
prejudice	evaluative definitions/ true religion

An alternative definition of religion

Of the seventeen definitions cited by Ferguson, none seems to escape completely the problems cited by Hall, Pilgrim and Cavanagh or by Barnhart. Hall, Pilgrim and Cavanagh, however, have offered an alternative definition of religion which they claim overcomes vagueness and narrowness by being specific and distinct and avoids compartmentalization and prejudice by including the whole of human life without judgement. According to Hall, Pilgrim and Cavanagh, therefore, *specificity* and *inclusiveness* characterize an adequate definition of religion.

In the light of these criteria, they offer the following alternative definition of religion: 'Religion is a varied, symbolic expression of, and appropriate response to, that which people deliberately affirm as being of unrestricted value for them' (1986, 11). Hall, Pilgrim and Cavanagh argue that this definition clearly outlines the subject matter of religion without excluding the wide variety of human symbols and conceptions of the unrestricted value. Moreover, they claim that this definition includes the many ways humans practice religion without evaluating any of those practices. Let us look carefully, therefore, at the various components within this definition.

Varied, symbolic expressions. By a symbol, Hall, Pilgrim and Cavanagh are referring to the ways in which humans communicate with, conceive of, and relate to, what they value without restriction. Symbols stand for, point to or represent the actual object which they symbolize. They occur in religious language, for example, through the telling of stories, the writing of sacred scriptures, the uttering of words in rituals, or by delineating confessions of faith. They are also seen in art, music and dance, in the patterns of a community's social organization, in ritual activities or in many combinations of these. A historian of religions, Charles Long (1986, 2), says that religious symbols 'radiate and deploy meanings' and that they therefore possess enormous power for any believing community.

People. For Hall, Pilgrim and Cavanagh, the term 'people' includes both individuals and communities, or what may be called the individual in the community (the I–We). The term 'people' (I–We) suggests that, initially, religion has something to do with the individual's quest for meaning denoted by such questions as 'Who am I?' 'Where did I come from?' or 'What will my end be?' Such questions, however, are articulated and answered in religion through believing communities as they develop what the scholar of comparative religions Wilfred Cantwell Smith (1978, 154) calls 'cumulative traditions'. The study of religion, therefore, is not just what individuals do with their solitariness (as Whitehead suggested) but also what communities as a whole do in response to basic human questions.

Deliberately affirm. Hall, Pilgrim and Cavanagh argue that religion is a human act which includes a voluntary choice. It is not capable of being reduced, therefore, to the study of the social sciences alone in which this act may be explained in terms of sociological functions or psychological needs. 'A person must intentionally embrace, accept, or affirm for him or herself the unrestricted value' (p. 13).

Unrestricted value. This refers to what the religious community prizes or esteems without limitation. It is the object towards which all the religious symbols of a community point; it embodies fundamental meaning itself. '"Unrestricted value" represents a judgment of importance that includes and surpasses every restricted, temporary, local or conditional value recognized in the relations constituting human experience' (p. 16).

Evaluating the Hall, Pilgrim and Cavanagh definition

Does the Hall, Pilgrim and Cavanagh definition of religion answer adequately our initial question 'What is religion?' Do we attain from them a clear and precise understanding of the field of our study? Are their own criteria satisfied by this definition? Initially, we must answer these questions in the negative since the Hall, Pilgrim and Cavanagh explanation fails at some points to overcome the errors they have identified in other definitions.

One problem in their definition results from their insistence that religion to be religion requires 'deliberate affirmation'. This commits the error of *narrowness* because it excludes religions which seem to place little value on individual choice or personal commitment. African traditional religions, for example, do not separate religious from non-religious activity. A person is 'religious' simply by being a part of the society. Hall, Pilgrim and Cavanagh's emphasis on deliberate affirmation, moreover, may reflect a Western bias (even a Protestant Christian attitude) which stresses that the individual *must affirm* the ultimate in order to be 'religious'.

The Hall, Pilgrim and Cavanagh definition of unrestricted value may also be accused of committing the error of *vagueness* or what Barnhart calls a *diluted definition.* The American sociologists Rodney Stark and William Bainbridge (1985, 5–7) would make such a complaint. Unrestricted value could include almost any human activity such as politics, sport, education, family life, scientific and technological research or many other areas of human life which some people regard as being of unlimited importance. For this reason, in contrast to Hall, Pilgrim and Cavanagh and to Barnhart, Stark and Bainbridge argue that religion to be religion must refer to some supernatural element.

Definitions such as the one offered by Hall, Pilgrim and Cavanagh suffer, in Stark and Bainbridge's opinion, from a Western bias held by many scholars earlier in this century that foresaw the eventual replacement of supernatural beliefs by scientific thinking (Berger, 1959, 13–42). Seemingly because they want to reserve a permanent place for religion in human life and because they fear that belief in the supernatural is not permanent, Hall, Pilgrim and Cavanagh have constructed a definition which would still allow religion to exist without the supernatural element because people will always use symbols to make deliberate affirmations of what they regard as being of unrestricted value.

Stark and Bainbridge object to this, asserting that 'there can be no wholly naturalistic religion'. They add, 'a religion lacking supernatural assumptions is no religion at all' (p. 3). If Stark and Bainbridge are right, therefore, not only do Hall, Pilgrim and Cavanagh commit their own error of vagueness but they (along with Barnhart) are wrong in their refusal to define religion as that which necessarily entails a belief in supernatural powers.

Towards a working definition of religion

The problems we have encountered defining religion demonstrate that we cannot attain a precise definition which will finally and perfectly delineate our field of study. We will need to accept, therefore, that any definition adopted can be a *working definition* only. By working definition I mean a definition which guides the student to identify data within human activities which might properly be included under the general heading of religious studies.

Ninian Smart (1986, 46–7), a contemporary scholar of religion, helps us develop such a working definition. He suggests that we must cease trying to develop precise definitions altogether since we will never be able to place what people have regarded as religious into one common category (theological, moral, philosophical, psychological or sociological). For example, some theological definitions which insist on beliefs in the supernatural as the essence of religion (such as that of Stark and Bainbridge) will exclude a large section of the Buddhist tradition which regards supernatural beings as irrelevant or even as impediments to the attainment of religious fulfilment. Yet almost every book on the world's religions includes this part of the Buddhist tradition as an example of 'religion'.

Smart suggests that one way we can overcome the problems inherent in defining religion is to study the religious traditions of humanity in terms of 'family resemblances'. All religions are related despite the fact that some forms of religion seem to have nothing in common with other forms. They are connected just as in a family where distant cousins may look nothing alike and may not even know of each other's existence but can still be traced to common ancestors through family interconnections. Following Smart, we can illustrate the interconnections between the religions (see Figure 1.1).

Figure 1.1:   THE INTERCONNECTIONS BETWEEN THE RELIGIONS

	PROPERTIES					
	A	B	C	D	E	F
Religion 1	X	X	X			
Religion 2		X	X	X		
Religion 3			X	X	X	
Religion 4				X	X	X

In this diagram, Religion 1 shares nothing in common with Religion 4. If one were looking for a common definition, it would be impossible to find one based on these two examples. But we see that Religion 1 shares two properties with Religion 2 (B and C) and one with Religion 3 (C) whereas Religion 4 shares two properties with Religion 3 (D and E) and one with Religion 2 (D). Through a series of connections, therefore, we can relate Religion 1 to Religion 4. In such a way, atheistic forms of Buddhism might form a part of religious studies just as monotheistic Islam would by finding common properties between them, for example, through Vedantic Hinduism and Zoroastrianism.

Although this way of approaching religious studies is not precise, it does explain why no universal definition of religion exists and the impossibility of creating such a definition. Nevertheless, Smart's approach is practical as it allows us to adopt a working definition which provides indicators or general guidelines for our field of study.

In the light of Smart's discussion, therefore, I would offer a slightly modified version of the Hall, Pilgrim and Cavanagh definition of religion as a working model to guide us in the direction of identifying religious data. Since 'deliberate affirmation' seems too narrow for certain traditions, such as in Africa, I would simply substitute 'that which people appropriately respond to' in its place as a broader description of what religious people are doing when they express themselves symbolically.

The concept of 'unrestricted value', moreover, can be retained if we understand the term as pointing towards that which transcends ordinary human experience. Although what transcends ordinary human experience need not reside beyond this world nor involve necessarily supernatural beings, it must in some sense transform that experience by bringing it into a dimension previously unknown and unknowable apart from the unrestricted value. This qualification accepts Stark and Bainbridge's critique without adopting their insistence on belief in the supernatural.

Thus our revised *working definition* of religion is as follows:

Religion is a varied, symbolic expression of that which people (the I-We) appropriately respond to as being of unrestricted value for them.

As we actually encounter religions, we may find this working definition imprecise, misleading, or even wrong in certain circumstances. The study of the phenomena, however, takes priority over attaining adequate definitions and thus, as the phenomena present themselves to the observer, the actual need for a definition will become less important.

Before moving to a description of phenomenology in response to the second preliminary question with which we began this chapter, we conclude this section by summarizing our revised version of the Hall, Pilgrim and Cavanagh working definition of religion in Figure 1.2 which incorporates Smart's idea of family resemblances.

What is phenomenology?

Phenomenology, in its twentieth century form, is a philosophical movement attributed to the German philosopher Edmund Husserl (1859-1938). Rather than offering descriptions of the nature of reality itself, it provides a method for knowing or investigating the way we know reality. The French phenomenologist, Maurice Merleau-Ponty, described phenomenology as a 'style of thinking' (cited by Bettis, 1969, 2), an effort to describe the actual state of affairs as disclosed by the phenomena of the world. In this section we explore briefly this style of thinking in order to understand how it has been applied to the study of religion. This topic will be more thoroughly discussed in Chapter Two.

Husserl's Phenomenology

Husserl did not invent the term phenomenology. Earlier German

Figure 1.2: A WORKING DEFINITION OF RELIGION INCORPORATING THE IDEA
OF 'FAMILY RESEMBLANCES'

Religion is . . .
1) A varied *symbolic expression*

	SYMBOLS					
	A	B	C	D	E	F
Religion 1	X	X	X			
Religion 2		X	X	X		
Religion 3			X	X	X	
Religion 4				X	X	X

2) of that which people *appropriately respond* to

	RESPONSE					
	A	B	C	D	E	F
Religion 1	X	X	X			
Religion 2		X	X	X		
Religion 3			X	X	X	
Religion 4				X	X	X

3) as being of *unrestricted value* for them

	PRECEPTION OF UNRESTRICTED VALUE					
	A	B	C	D	E	F
Religion 1	X	X	X			
Religion 2		X	X	X		
Religion 3			X	X	X	
Religion 4				X	X	X

philosophers, such as G.W.F. Hegel in his *Phenomenology of Spirit* (1807), employed the term, as did Johann Gottlieb Fichte, writing in 1804, who used it as a tool for interpreting states of the consciousness, the English translation of his book entitled *Facts of Consciousness* (Copleston, 1965a, 53). Later, the German philosopher Hermann Lotze investigated the soul as a phenomenological term and Eduard von Hartmann referred to the phenomenology of religious consciousness (Höffding, 1950, 520–524, 533–537).

It is incorrect, therefore, to associate phenomenology strictly with Edmund Husserl. Nevertheless, the way in which he interpreted philosophical questions underlies almost all later phenomenologies, including the German school comprised, among others, of Max Scheler, Nicolai Hartmann and Martin Heidegger (1982) and the French existentialists including Gabriel Marcel, Jean-Paul Sartre, Paul Ricour, and as we have noted, Maurice Merleau-Ponty (Ayer, 1982, 214–233, Spielberg, 1982, 7–12).

Before exploring how Husserl delineated the phenomenological method for obtaining knowledge, I will define three key concepts beneath his approach: rigorous science, philosophical radicalism and intentionality.

Rigorous Science. Husserl's original field was mathematics from which he learned the precision of methodological clarity. He believed that the science of the early twentieth century had degenerated into the unphilosophical study of mere facts — what can be known through direct observations (often referred to as positivism). Scientific enquiry had also become dominated by a related concept called 'naturalism' which explained the world exclusively in terms of apparent natural occurrences thereby leaving no room for seeing into 'meanings' beneath the phenomena of nature.

The incapacity, and even unwillingness, of science to explore problems of value and meaning because of its confinement to positive facts defined for Husserl what he called 'the crisis of science' (1965, 191–192). Husserl, however, did not reject the natural sciences as legitimate fields of study. Rather, he regarded them as needing the assistance of a rigorous science based on clearly articulated philosophical methods aimed at perceiving an underlying systematic order (Bréhier, 1969, 210).

Philosophical radicalism. Radical means 'going to the roots'. The roots of knowledge for Husserl begin with the objects or things of perception, what he called the phenomena (from the Greek word *phanos*, meaning 'that which manifests itself'). Although the phenomena comprise the ground for all human concepts, knowledge does not dwell in the things themselves but in the consciousness of the knowing subject. By employing a proper methodology within the consciousness (which I explain below), the observer uncovers a correlation between the subjective awareness (the act of perceiving) and the objects perceived (the content of perception) (Copleston, 1965b, 207-210; Spiegelberg, 1982, 77).

Intentionality. Intentionality refers to the act of perceiving and understanding the phenomena. It implies that the observer actively directs his attention towards an object. Perception, therefore, for Husserl, did not consist of the subject passively receiving impressions on his blank consciousness. The subject rather intentionally interacts with the objects of perception and integrates them into his mind. The act of cognition thus is comprised of directing subjective intentions toward intentional objects thereby making them genuinely objective (Smith, 1983, 249–286; Bréhier, 1969, 207–208).

Within the framework of a rigorous science and in the light of philosophical radicalism, therefore, intentionality overcomes the tendency of positivism to define knowledge as limited to passively receiving mere facts and it ensures that meanings are discerned beneath acts of observation.

Husserl's description of the phenomenological method

Husserl defined the phenomenological method as a descriptive theory of knowledge (Merleau-Ponty, 1969, 14). It begins from within the person, the subject, and seeks to move outside the person into an objective description of the world (intentionality). In this process, nothing can be assumed or presupposed. Following from his philosophical radicalism, everything, even the existence of the external world, must be questioned. The purpose of this is to describe the phenomena and to attain an understanding of that which is manifested.

As we noted in his call for a rigorous science, Husserl conceived his original task as clarifying the concepts of logic and mathematics and how they relate to thought processes (Allen, 1985, 255–62).This led him to assert a 'necessary essence' to mathematical and logical formulae. Thus if we take the simple mathematical statement $2 + 2 = 4$, we know that the specific class of objects being referred to can vary. We could speak of two bananas being equal to four bananas or of two pencils plus two pencils being equal to four pencils. We could also insert into the formula the subject's moods, emotions or personal perceptions. Despite the various classifications of objects and the subjective states of the observer, an essence or essential quality of this formula remains constant (Hirschberger, 1976, 194).

The same type of essence as is found in a mathematical formula corresponds to objects in the world itself (Husserl, 1978, 119). To attain an understanding of these essences, the observer must suspend his previous judgements about the world, including his own feelings, ideas and presuppositions, and attempt to see into the very essence of the phenomena themselves. To do this, the observer must execute two key activities.

He must first perform what Husserl calls *epochē* (from the Greek, meaning 'to stop' or 'to hold back') (Sharpe, 1986, 224). All of his thoughts about material things, science, other humans, the sequence and order of events, or any other presuppositions must be suspended or, to use a term Husserl borrowed from mathematics, 'put into brackets'. By 'bracketing out' every previously held belief or assumption, the observer allows the pure phenomena to speak for themselves.

The second key activity for the phenomenologist can now occur. The observer performs the eidetic intuition whereby only the essential structures of the phenomena are seen. The eidetic intuition (from the Greek word *eidos* meaning form, idea or essence) allows the observer to see into the very structure or meaning of the phenomena.

Intuition suggests that the bracketed consciousness of one who has performed *epochē* is able to apprehend not just particular entities or even universal classes of entities (such as particular bananas and then 'bananahood', what makes a banana a banana), but their *essential meanings* as entities and classes of entities. This can occur only when one's preconceived notions are suspended thereby enabling the observer to intuit the meaning of what actually manifests itself in the world. This is why the eidetic intuition is also called the eidetic vision — seeing into the very nature or meaning of what exists in the world (Bettis, 1969, 10). Husserl ([1913] 1978, 246) explains,

> The multiplicity of possible perceptions, memories, and, indeed, intentional processes of whatever sort, that relate, or can relate, 'harmoniously' to one and the same physical thing has (in all its tremendous complication) a quite definite *essential style*.

This combination of *epochē* and the eidetic intuition is required for the building up of an objective picture of the phenomena of existence. *Epochē* allows the observer to call into question his own presuppositions, unchallenged assumptions and biases and also to call into question any other theories of knowledge — no matter how compelling they may appear or how widely they may be held. This means, moreover, suspending any prior judgement about what is real or apparent, true or false. The observer thus perceives the world as it comes fresh from the phenomena and is able thereby to intuit new realities or at least achieve a more complete understanding of reality than had been previously attained.

Application of the method

Epochē and the eidetic intuition are the primary tools whereby the phenomenologist sees into the structures of existence and thus builds an objective description of the world. As the observer intuits essences and allows the phenomena to speak for themselves, three basic steps occur: naming objects, noting relations, describing processes.

Naming objects. In the condition of the bracketed consciousness, the observer will perceive a variety of phenomena which he will need to distinguish from one another by giving names to them. Although the names are not identical with the phenomena themselves, by naming objects, the observer makes sense of what appears. Hence, we name stones, houses, trees, books and all the other multitude of things which form the phenomena of our experience. Naming the phenomena enables us to speak intelligibly about that which has manifested itself to our consciousness.

Noting relations. We need not only name the objects of the phenomena, we also begin to understand relations between them from very simple to complex concepts. If we watch birds flying, for example, we may just note the relationship between one bird and another. But if we see birds flying quickly and nervously as the skies darken and we hear distant thunder, we will form logical and temporal relations associating the actions of the birds with an impending storm. As we build relations between the named objects, we are forming structures of reality based on our observations of the phenomena themselves.

Describing processes. The observer will also begin to describe processes at work within the phenomena. These include processes like development as, for example, when one sees a plant grow in response to proper amounts of sunlight and water. Processes in history may be observed as each event creates or influences later events. Psychological processes may be described as people go through stages, for example, from fear through anger to remorse.

By naming objects, noting relationships and describing processes, the phenomenologist claims to build the structure of reality not from presuppositions about the world but from the observed phenomena themselves. This is a method of 'getting inside' the phenomena through *epoche* in order to see into the essence of them. Although the starting point of philosophical phenomenology is subjective, its goal is to describe and understand the world objectively (Merleau-Ponty, 1969, 27–8).

The objectivity obtainable through this method, however, can only approximate reality and thus can never be final or exact —particularly when it is applied to the human sciences. Humans are always changing and thus constitute a special type of phenomenon. This fact becomes apparent, for example, when phenomenology is applied to religion. The results of the method, therefore, must always remain incomplete and open to revision.

The need for openness to revision, however, does not detract from the method but forms an inevitable part of it. When an observer intuits the essence or structure of objects, relations and processes, his conclusions always remain accountable to the phenomena. In other words, the method always calls the phenomenologist back to the source of his knowledge. Any eidetic intuition, therefore, must be tested and revised in the light of the phenomena. This guarantees that the essence is not, in the words of J. Hirshberger, 'a mere universal' but a 'self-validating *eidos*' (p. 194).

Summary of the method

A summary (following Husserl) of how the phenomenological method obtains knowledge of the world is shown in the following steps:
Epochē
1. Suspend judgements, bracket previous theories, opinions, ideas or thoughts.
2. Disregard prior distinctions between the real and apparent, true or false.
3. Allow the phenomena to speak for themselves within the bracketed consciousness.
Eidetic intuition
4. Build structures of meaning by naming objects, noting relationships and describing processes within the phenomena.
5. Intuit the essential meanings of the phenomena from their structures.
Testing the intuition
6. Test the intuition by going back to the phenomena, making adjustments where necessary.

Limitations of the method

The student should be reminded that philosophical phenomenology chiefly examines the role of the subjective observer in apprehending the objective world. As a method of knowing, it recognizes that perceptions of the world are limited by and inseparable from the intentionality of the observer, in the technical philosophical sense of the term as employed by Husserl. This guards against charges that the method reflects a naive form of sensationalism whereby the subject merely experiences and takes note of various phenomena striking his bracketed consciousness. As implied in Husserl's key concepts beneath phenomenology, *epoche* does not remove the observer from the *act* of observing.

Merleau-Ponty (1986, 3–4) cautioned against minimizing the role of the perceiver in the act of perception through his assertion that 'nothing in our experience' corresponds to 'pure sensation'. He offered the following example to demonstrate this point.

> Let us imagine a white patch on a homogeneous background. All the points in the patch have a certain 'function' in common, that of forming

themselves into a 'shape'. The colour of the shape is more intense and, as it were, more resistant than that of the background; the edges of the white patch 'belong' to it, and are not part of the background though they adjoin it: the patch appears to be placed on the background and does not break it up. Each part arouses the expectation of more than it contains, and this elementary perception is therefore already charged with *a meaning*.

This example demonstrates that performing *epochē* does not eliminate the fundamentally active role of the observer in describing phenomena. Nevertheless, it shows that the phenomenon itself provides the source of and criterion for the observations recorded. As such, the method seeks to reduce the impact of pre-judgements on the consciousness of the observer so that he may intuit meanings contained in the phenomena, their relationships and their processes.

Moreover, the student should understand that the *eidos* or essence of the phenomena primarily provides a means for understanding how the observer interacts with the data of experience and is not an end in itself. This point warns the student against assuming that the aim of phenomenology is to discover a final content or an unchanging universal idea. Rather, the method aims at understanding how the consciousness interacts with the phenomena. Merleau-Ponty (1986, xvi–xvii) explains: 'The world is not what I think, but what I live through. I am open to the world, I have no doubt that I am in communication with it, but I do not possess it: it is inexhaustible.'

Two fundamental limitations must be noted, therefore, within the method: no 'pure' descriptions of the phenomena separable from the subjective observer are attainable; and no final or universal statement of the essence of the meaning of the world is possible. These two limitations result from the phenomenological analysis of the interaction of the subject with the objective world and will remain important considerations when we discuss the application of the phenomenological method to religion.

Conclusions

We have now arrived at a working definition of religion and have outlined the meaning of phenomenology from a philosophical perspective. The student should be able, therefore, to respond to the two questions with which we began this chapter: What is religion? and What is phenomenology?

In response to the first question, the student should now recognize the complexity involved in defining religion and should appreciate that our suggested working definition operates merely as a flexible indicator of what we are studying in the field of religion. Moreover, the content of the study will become meaningful only as we fill it with real phenomena obtained from the actual experiences of believing communities. At this point the student can respond to the second question simply by describing a philosophical method for obtaining knowledge. This method, like the working definition of religion, must be filled with actual phenomena in order for it to come to life. In the next chapter, I endeavour to describe how this can be done by applying the phenomenological method to the study of human religious practice.

References

ALLEN, D. 1985 *Philosophy for Understanding Theology* (London, SCM Press).

AYER, A.J. 1982 *Philosophy in the Twentieth Century* (London, Heidenfeld and Nicolson).

BARNHART, J. E. 1977 *The Study of Religion and its Meaning* (The Hague, Mouton).

BERGER, P. L. 1969 *A Rumour of Angels* (London, Penguin).

BETTIS, J. D. 1969 *Phenomenology of Religion* (New York, Harper and Row).

BRÉHIER, E. 1969 *Contemporary Philosophy - since 1850*, trans. W. Baskin (Chicago and London, University of Chicago Press).

COPLESTON, F. 1965a *A History of Philosophy, Volume 7, Part I: Fichte to Hegel* (Garden City, New York, Image Books).

COPLESTON, F. 1965b *A History of Philosophy, Volume 7, Part II: Schopenhauer to Nietzsche* (Garden City, New York, Image Books).

FERGUSON, J. 1978 *Religions of the World* (Guildford, Lutterworth).

HALL, T. W., R. B. PILGRIM and R. R. CAVANAGH 1986 *Religion: An Introduction* (San Francisco, Harper and Row).

HEGEL, G.W.F. [1807] 1977 *Phenomenology of Spirit*, trans. A.V. Miller (Oxford, Oxford University Press).

HEIDEGGER, M. [1975] 1982 *The Basic Problems of Phenomenology*, trans. A. Hofstadter (Bloomington, Indiana University Press).

HIRSCHBERGER, J. 1976 *A Short History of Western Philosophy* (Guildford, Lutterworth).

HÖFFDING, H. [1900] 1950 *A History of Modern Philosophy, trans. B.E. Meyer* (New York, The Humanities Press).

HUSSERL, E. [1913] 1978 *Formal and Transcendental Logic*, trans. D. Cairns (The Hague, Martinus Nijhoff).

HUSSERL, E. 1965 'Philosophy as a rigorous science', trans. Q. Lauer, in Husserl, E. *Phenomenology and the Crisis of Philosophy* (New York, Harper and Row).

LESSA, W. and E. VOGT 1965 *Reader in Comparative Religion: An Anthropological Approach* (New York, Harper and Row).

LONG, C. 1986 *Significations: Signs, Symbols and Images in the Interpretation of Religion* (Philadelphia, Fortress).

MERLEAU-PONTY, M. 1969 'What is phenomenology of religion?', in J. D. Bettis (ed.), *Phenomenology of Religion* (New York, Harper and Row).

MERLEAU-PONTY, M. 1986 *Phenomenology of Perception*, trans. C. Smith (London, Routledge).

PROZESKY, M. 1984 *Religion and Ultimate Well-being* (London, Macmillan).

SHARPE, E. 1986 *Comparative Religion: A History* (London, Duckworth).

SMART, N. 1986 *Concept and Empathy: Essays in the Study of Religion*, ed. D. Wiebe (London, Macmillan).

Smith, D.W. 1983 'Husserl's philosophy of mind', in Floistad, G (ed.), *Contemporary Philosophy: A New Survey. Vol. 4: Philosophy of Mind* (The Hague, Martinus Nijhoff), 249-286.

SMITH, W. C. 1978 *The Meaning and End of Religion* (San Francisco, Harper and Row).

SPIEGELBERG, H. 1982 *The Phenomenological Movement* (The Hague, Martinus NIjhoff).

STARK, R. and W. BAINBRIDGE 1985 *The Future of Religion: Secularization, Revival and Cult Formation* (Berkeley and Los Angeles, Univ. of California Press).

Questions and activities

Questions for discussion

1. Evaluate each definition of religion listed by Ferguson according to the criteria of Hall, Pilgrim and Cavanagh. Do the same for Barnhart's criteria. Do you note any difference between those of Hall, Pilgrim and Cavanagh and those of Barnhart?

2. Evaluate the Hall, Pilgrim and Cavanagh definition of religion according to their own criteria. List weaknesses and strengths of their definition.

3. What does Smart mean by 'family resemblances'? Try to give examples of how this might apply in the study of actual religions. How does this help us develop a working definition of religion?

4. Of the seventeen definitions of religion given by Ferguson, which could fit into more than one classification? List each of your choices under the various categories and then justify your choices.

5. Does religion require a belief in the supernatural to qualify as a religion? Why or why not?

6. What is the meaning of *epochē* and how could it apply to the presuppositions which people hold about their experience in the world?

7. What are phenomena? List some of them.

8. Identify relationships between the phenomena given in your answer to Question 7. Do these relationships exist in the phenomena themselves? If not, where do they come from?

9. Describe what it means to see into the essence of a phenomenon. Give examples.

10. In the light of your answer to Question 9, is it correct to call phenomenology a method of knowing rather than a comment on reality? Why or why not?

Projects and activities

1. Write your own definition of religion and then evaluate it according to the criteria presented in this chapter.

2. Define what you personally consider to be of unrestricted value. Does this require a deliberate affirmation? Describe ways you symbolize it. Do others also affirm this value? Is your unrestricted value 'supernatural'?

3. Attend a religious gathering of a group of which you are not a member. Describe what symbols are used to affirm the unrestricted value. From your observations, what do you understand the unrestricted value of this community to be?

4. Find a place where you can be alone. Perform *epochē*. Allow the phenomena to strike your consciousness in its suspended condition. Do this for at least twenty minutes without losing concentration. Write a five-page essay summarizing what you experienced. Include in your essay an analysis of how your mind organized the phenomena.

5. Follow the procedure in Project 4, but for shorter intervals, for 14 days. Keep a daily diary in which you name the phenomena perceived, describe relationships between them as they strike your consciousness, and list any processes involved. At the end of the two weeks, write a summary of what you learned from the experience.

Chapter Two
The Phenomenology of Religion

If we simply combine the two answers of the previous chapter, we will arrive at a preliminary definition of what the phenomenology of religion entails: the phenomenology of religion is a method adapting the procedures of *epochē* and eidetic intuition to the study of the varied symbolic expressions of that which people appropriately respond to as being of unrestricted value for them.

The phenomenology of religion, however, is more than a compilation of these two definitions. For all scholars in the field, it has comprised an orderly method for the study of religion. Historically, attempts to correct some of the weaknesses in the presentations of earlier phenomenologists were attempted by those writing later, as was done, for example, by C.J. Bleeker of Gerardus van der Leeuw (Bleeker, 1971, 9-29).

I have not followed the historical development of the method in this chapter. For this approach, the student is referred to Eric Sharpe's *Comparative Religion: A History* (1986). I have chosen rather to present the method in a step-by-step format based on the writings of some leading twentieth-century phenomenologists.

The stages explained in this chapter, however, should not be regarded as dictating how every phenomenologist has employed the method. Rather, they represent how I have interpreted the key elements in the phenomenology of religion. As such, they do not constitute *the* steps in the phenomenological method in any absolute sense. I have arranged the components of the method in stages to assist students in understanding how the method can work practically and to outline it in a systematic fashion. The presentation in this chapter, therefore, follows closely the principal concepts employed by phenomenologists of religion, but it should be observed as a practical guideline rather than as a fixed prescription.

The application of the method to the study of religion

Step 1. Performing epochē

Just as with philosophical phenomenology, the phenomenologist of religion begins by suspending or bracketing his previous ideas, thoughts, opinions or beliefs. This means suspending *personal beliefs* and withholding judgements on *academic theories* about religion. The phenomenologist wants to observe the phenomena of religion as they appear rather than as they are understood through opinions formed prior to observation. The suspension of personal beliefs requires that the phenomenologist bracket out his own views about religious truth or practice. If, for example, the observer is a committed Christian who believes that Jesus Christ is the true and complete revelation of God, he must suspend that judgement and try to allow the phenomena he is observing to speak for themselves without their being filtered through his Christian presuppositions. Or, if the observer is an atheist who denies the reality of any supernatural force, the same suspension of judgement must be performed if the phenomena are not to be distorted by the observer's preconceived ideas.

Academic theories about the nature, function, purpose or meaning of religion must also be suspended or bracketed. For example, the Freudian claim that religion is a universal obsessive neurosis, whether true or false, must be held in abeyance in order that the religious phenomena may manifest themselves to the observer without distortion. Other academic presuppositions from many fields such as sociology, anthropology, ethnology, geography, politics, economics and so on must be placed in brackets in order that they do not interfere with the integrity of the phenomena as they appear to the observer.

One of the most influential phenomenologists of religion earlier in the twentieth century was the Dutch scholar Gerardus van der Leeuw who was Professor of the History of Religion at the University of Groningen. His famous book, *Religion in Essence and Manifestation* (1938), employs many of Husserl's concepts including the initial step of performing *epochē*.

In a book outlining the phenomenology of religion, Olaf Pettersson and Hans Akerberg (1981, 26) suggest that Husserl's definition of *epochē* as 'the exclusion from one's mind of every possible presupposition' was used in religious studies by van der Leeuw in order to gain a 'relationship of understanding between the subject and the object'. A central problem for the study of religion is how the subjective observer gains knowledge of an objective entity when that objective entity (religious life and practice) is embodied in subjective experience. Hence van der Leeuw recognized that the problem of understanding entails the need for 'scholars to see the object both in its internal structure and its broader connections'. *Epochē*, for van der Leeuw, enables the observer to attain understanding of the subjective nature of religion (its internal structure) and its objective meaning (its broader connections).

W. Brede Kristensen was another early phenomenologist who adopted the method of *epochē* in order that the central aim of understanding religion could be achieved. For Kristensen, this occurs only when the scholar is able to see through the viewpoint or perspective of the adherents since 'there is no religious reality other than the faith of the believers' (cited by Platvoet, 1990, 34).

Kristensen, therefore, saw *epochē* as a method or a tool whereby the observer could avoid value judgements. He believed that evolutionary theories in particular (to which we will return in the next chapter) predisposed the scholar to evaluate religions from the outside and thus, in the words of a historian of comparative religions, Eric Sharpe, 'to have been responsible for inducing scholars to pass premature judgment on material they had learned to understand only in part' (Sharpe, 1986, 228).

In van der Leeuw and Kristensen, therefore, we meet two phenomenologists who represent the larger phenomenological reaction against distorting the testimony of the believers through the observer's preconceived ideas or theories. Husserl's method of *epochē* thus provided a useful first step to avoid pre-judging the phenomena in order that an understanding of religion from the inside might be attained.

The initial stage of *epochē*, however, should not be regarded as an effort to remove the observer from interacting creatively with the phenomena. In fact, as we noted from van der Leeuw, one of the purposes of performing *epochē* is to enable him to do so. But this interaction inevitably brings with it a number of problems which to some degree limit the method itself.

For example, in any description of religious activity, the observer must select which aspects are important and which are not. A certain emphasis results from this selection which later influences the understanding of the religious activity itself. This problem has been noted by Pettersson and Akerberg (1981, 14) who call it one of the fundamental limitations of *epochē*. They ask, 'What unitary principles or concepts direct the selections of data and what factors determine the interpretation of the data?'

Moreover, even though the observer endeavours to suspend all previous judgements, this is probably impossible since each person brings with him cultural, social and psychological understandings which are in part hidden to his consciousness. These understandings have influenced him since birth and reflect his own time in history. Pettersson and Akerberg suggest that 'the scholar is to a great extent committed to the ideas of his age. When he begins his studies, he is already influenced' (p. 61).

Epochē, therefore, cannot be practised perfectly and is best understood as an *attitude towards* religious phenomena which recognizes and admits that the scholar begins from certain perspectives and predispositions. The attitude sought is to try to minimize the observer's admitted and recognized preconceptions in order that a fresh look at religious phenomena may yield new insights and achieve greater understanding. But the student should be aware from the outset that performing *epochē* can occur only within limits because the observer, by definition, plays an active role in phenomenological descriptions.

Step 2. Performing empathetic interpolation

This step is related closely to the performing *epochē*. After the observer has suspended his own judgements, he must 'enter into' the experience of the believing community he is studying. If the phenomena are to be described with a minimal amount of distortion they cannot be merely observed: they must be understood. This corresponds to what Husserl meant by 'getting inside' the phenomena of experience. The phenomenologist of religion must 'get inside' the religion he is studying and view the world, as far as possible, as a believer does.

The scholar of comparative religions Wilfred Cantwell Smith argues forcefully for this approach (1978, 51–79). He contends that religion is not a 'thing' and that observable faith cannot be objectified or, as he calls it, 'reified'. Faith, which is expressed through observable phenomena, is intensely personal. To describe any phenomenon from the outside, therefore, is to make it something unrecognizable to the believer. If it is unrecognizable to the believer, it surely cannot portray accurately what it is in itself.

But 'getting inside' a religion is not easy. Barriers of culture, language and unexplained symbols may make the task extremely difficult. This is why the phenomenologist first needs to employ empathy, the cultivation of a feeling for the religious life of the community he is seeking to understand. This 'feeling for' requires him to identify with the attitudes, thoughts and activities of the believers. It does not mean that the phenomenologist personally becomes a believer since that would move him from empathy to conversion. But the phenomenologist must foster the empathetic attitude of identification by trying to see into and through the mind of the adherent.

Since an empathetic attitude does not guarantee understanding, the phenomenologist must also interpolate what may seem strange or unusual in the religion he is studying into what is meaningful to him. To interpolate means to insert what is outside one's experience into one's experience by translating that which is foreign into what is familiar.

Van der Leeuw first coined the term 'sympathetic interpolation' in his description of the stages in the phenomenological method. Ninian Smart (1973, 54) prefers the term 'empathetic' to describe the way in which the observer is able to recognize 'a framework of intentions' among the believers. Intentionality thus not only requires the active involvement of the observer but also includes the acts of a believing community (what it intends by its myths, rituals and symbols), which must be apprehended by the observer if he is to understand what he is actually observing.

Wilfred Cantwell Smith's popular book *The Faith of Other Men* (1972) offers a classic example of empathetic interpolation. Smith admits that for the Westerner many of the religions of the world seem strange and incomprehensible. He therefore endeavours to translate some of those seemingly incomprehensible concepts by interpolating them into the lives of ordinary Westerners. He does this, for example, with the Hindu statement '*tat tvam asi* ', which means 'that thou art' (pp. 24–38).

For the Vedantic Hindu, this terse phrase points towards a deep religious truth which affirms the unity of the individual soul with the universal world spirit. Smith attempts to interpolate this for the Western mind by suggesting that in art, morality and theology people seek a correspondence between what they appreciate aesthetically, do morally or believe ultimately and what *really is* Beautiful, Good, and True. This awareness of the unity between individual experiences and the universal, says Smith, empathetically interpolates what the Westerner has often perceived as enigmatic within the Hindu tradition.

The step of empathetic interpolation, like *epochē*, however, should be regarded as imprecise and hence more like an attitude than an empirically measurable method. The observer 'cultivates a feeling for' the religious experience of a believer but can never experience precisely what a believer experiences. Moreover, interpolation always approximates what it might feel like to be a believer in terms of one's own life and culture. Such a manœuvre is quite subject to misinterpretation and thus the student should be warned against applying it too casually.

In addition, since this step in the method does not use the tools of empirical observation strictly but consciously endeavours to adopt an attitude towards religious phenomena, limitations to accuracy inevitably result. Pettersson and Akerberg note that this procedure employs psychological methods because, by definition, the empirical data the scholar seeks to understand is inner experience: 'The situation is, then, that one person — the scholar — wants to understand another person's religion. To reach this he must abandon the strictly historical method which does not answer questions about understanding' (1981, 61).

Van der Leeuw sought to resolve this problem by arguing that all science requires interpretation, and hence, unless one wants to abandon all efforts to achieve understanding, hermeneutics (the art of interpretation) is inevitable in all empirical studies (Pettersson and Akerberg, p. 61). That the need for interpretation is accentuated in the scholar's effort to understand religious experience should not be surprising and certainly should not invalidate the method. It does serve, however, to help students of religion become aware of the limitations in applying this stage in the method.

Step 3. Maintaining epochē

Because Step 2 is one of empathetic interpolation rather than conversion, the act of *epochē* is maintained throughout. This means that by entering into another religion the phenomenologist does not now believe what the adherent believes. The religious community he seeks to understand may hold many beliefs about the ultimate reality or about the nature of human society, but the phenomenologist maintains his suspension of judgement about these beliefs.

Ninian Smart (1973, 56) argues that 'phenomenology "brackets" questions of theological truth'. After citing many problems connected with the process and related to the intentions of the believers, he calls the maintaining of *epochē* the suspending of judgements on everything which the believer uses to 'express' the object of his faith (such as doctrines and myths) and everything which he thinks 'manifests' that faith (those events or signs which the adherent affirms as making the object of faith apparent).

C. Jouco Bleeker, who was Professor of the History of Religions at the University of Amsterdam during the 1960s, underscored the need to maintain *epochē*. Bleeker (1963, 3) insisted that phenomenology 'cannot concern itself with the truth of religion' but must nevertheless treat each religion with respect, empathy and seriousness. Bleeker asserted that phenomenology 'maintains its position of impartiality' by refusing to pass judgements on the beliefs of any religion. Phenomenology simply recognizes such beliefs as 'a serious testimony of religious people that they possess a knowledge of God' (p. 9).

Therefore, the truth or falsehood of the beliefs of any religious community is not considered by the phenomenologist. This corresponds to the rejection by philosophical phenomenology of the distinction between what is real and what is apparent. What is important for the phenomenologist of religion is not what is true, but an accurate description and an understanding of what the adherent believes to be true; what the phenomenologist personally believes has already been 'bracketed out'.

But the issue of 'truth' also raises problems and indicates limitations in the method. The contemporary scholar Donald Wiebe (1981, 1–6), for example, distinguishes between the truth 'of' religion and the truth 'about' religion. Wiebe argues that phenomenology has endeavoured to bracket the truth 'of' religion while seeking to describe the truth 'about' religion. But this very distinction may be an alien concept to many adherents and may be objectionable to them. It may implicitly contradict, therefore, the idea of empathetic interpolation. One could argue quite successfully that the truth 'of' religion is quite central to a Christian or a Muslim whereas what a phenomenologist might describe as the truth 'about' their religions might (potentially at least) clash with their faith commitments.

To maintain *epochē* about the truth claims of any religion, therefore, requires a distancing of the observer from the perspectives of the adherent. This indicates a tension between 'cultivating a feeling for' the testimony of the believers at Step 2 and suspending all judgements about the claims of the believers at Step 3.

In his discussion of this issue, Smart (1973, 33–4) has offered a solution through the procedure of 'expressive bracketing' in which students of religious phenomena incorporate 'expressions' into their 'descriptions'. In other words, the scholar of religion seeks to describe evocatively the feelings, tones, attitudes and convictions of the believer. By placing these in brackets, Smart argues, the phenomenologist can portray 'what a situation is like' without committing himself personally to the content of that situation, to the practices it encourages, or to the feelings it induces. This method enables the observer to imagine what it would be like to be a believer or to act 'as if' he were one.

Smart admits that 'expressive bracketing' can be 'misleading' and must be understood in the context of seeking to describe and understand objectively what is at its core a subjective experience. Nevertheless, expressive bracketing makes some progress toward maintaining *epochē* while endeavouring at the same time to portray accurately and with empathy the faith commitments of believers.

Step 4. Describing the phenomena

In his observations of the activities of any religious group and by his 'getting inside' them, the phenomenologist will encounter a wide variety of religious data. His first task in this process is to describe the data as accurately as possible, paying careful attention to the various aspects so as to avoid premature interpretations. Words, actions, gestures, songs, symbols, explanations by adherents and so on must be recorded in detail. Moreover, the descriptions obtained must correspond as faithfully as possible to the believers' own testimony. Following Brede Kristensen (1969, 48–9) on this point, the phenomenological method seeks to be fair to the adherent's perspective in the conviction that the final authority is not the observer but the believer.

In practical terms, however, it should be noted that no 'pure' descriptions are possible as this stage also includes a strong attitudinal component on the part of the observer. The student of religion endeavours to describe accurately what is occurring, but it can never be forgotten that he is the one doing the observing, interviewing, recording and transmitting of religious data.

This involves a process of selecting relevant material, organizing that material meaningfully, emphasizing or ignoring aspects within the phenomena, selecting subjects for interviews and composing questionnaires. Although the scholar may try to present the data as a believer would, his own judgements will inevitably influence his descriptions. Moreover, as

Smart has noted, the observer must not only describe occurrences but must also convey feelings, moods and tones within phenomena which makes it even more difficult for him to attain objectivity.

Within limits, however, the student of religion can follow Kristensen's ideal of endeavouring to make descriptions consistent with the perspectives of believers and then to devise ways to test the descriptions among believing communities. This stage in the method thus involves an attitude of fairness on the part of the observer, but it must not be employed under the illusion that it can produce 'pure' objectivity. Observations require creative interaction by the scholar with religious data which, despite its essential creativity, can be characterized by an effort to portray as accurately as possible what is actually occurring in the phenomena.

Step 5. Naming the phenomena

After describing a variety of phenomena within a particular community, the phenomenologist of religion will follow a similar pattern to that of the philosophical phenomenologist who builds the structure of existence from his perceptions of the phenomena. The structure of religion can be derived only after the assigning of names or categories to similar types of phenomena described at Step 4. Selecting the names depends on two factors: avoiding distortion and making sense of the religious phenomena.

To avoid distortion, descriptive categories of types of phenomena should be as value-free as possible. Some words, although not wrong in themselves, carry connotations which misrepresent the actual meaning for the believer. The phenomenologist, therefore, must be aware of the danger of creating names which prejudice his descriptions.

For example, indigenous religions such as African traditional religions have been called 'primitive', 'basic', 'pre-literate', or 'local'. These words, although not necessarily inaccurate from an outsider's point of view, misconstrue the perceptions of the religious communities themselves. Other examples of words commonly used to name religious phenomena which carry distorting connotations include 'animism', 'superstition', 'magic', 'caste system', 'witchcraft' and 'sorcery'.

In this book, following Hall, Pilgrim and Cavanagh's definition of religion, I suggest the following categories for the naming of the phenomena: 'myths', 'rituals', 'sacred practitioners', 'scripture', 'art', 'morality' and 'beliefs'. These broad classifications of the phenomena can be divided further as, for example, between cosmogonic and socio-moral myths. But each category seeks to be faithful to the phenomena without distorting what a believer within any tradition would be willing to affirm.

In any religious community, therefore, a phenomenologist, after describing the data, will place them within one of the categories and then, where appropriate, into subcategories. This is done initially for the purpose of clarifying the phenomena in order that the observer may understand them. The naming of a specific phenomenon, however, also requires the phenomenologist to perceive a more general pattern in the actions observed. From his description of myths, for example, the roles, functions, and types of myths can be discerned from the various ways they are used in one tradition and perhaps also in others. Following van der Leeuw, Smart (1973, 47) calls this the development of 'typological descriptions' which he defines as 'an inventory of types of religious items', aspects of which include 'doctrines, myths, ethics, rituals, experiences, and institutions'.

Eric Sharpe (1971, 46) offers an excellent description of how this operates:

> Prayer is an ideal case in point. Wherever prayer is found, it may be studied. It should be studied precisely as it is found, without manipulation and rationalization, as a mode of communication with the deity. The question of the existence or otherwise of the deity is left open, as is the problem of the efficacy of prayer. The student attempts by this method to discover the function of prayer in various religions.

By discerning types or patterns of various religious activities within one tradition, the scholar can identify similar types in other traditions. Brede Kristensen called this 'informative comparison' which, as Richard Plantinga (1989, 175) explains, requires the scholar 'in order to understand given phenomena' to 'compare similar phenomena in different religious traditions, even if they are historically unrelated'.

If the phenomenological method were to stop at this point, however, it would be vulnerable to the criticism, in Pettersson's and Akerberg's words, that it overlooks 'not only the historical but the cultural context'. This means that the phenomenological classifications and their interpretations of types across religious traditions would be done 'independently of any historical or cultural systemization' (p. 14).

The student should be aware when applying this stage in the method that the names or classifications which he assigns to his observations are related to specific traditions which operate within definitive cultures and which possess unique histories. It is necessary, however, to name the phenomena in order to discuss them meaningfully in common discourse and to attain interpretations of their meaning. As we shall see shortly, the phenomenological method accommodates the need to recognize historical and cultural processes at the next step.

At this point, however, we need to underscore once again a consistent, but unavoidable, limitation within the phenomenological method. This limitation becomes evident as soon as the scholar begins to assign names to the phenomena. He soon realizes that he can do this only after having formed some prior assumptions on the basis of knowledge he has already attained. For example, he must already have some idea of what he means by prayer before he names this activity and clarifies its meaning for the tradition he is studying. In the first instance, this awareness cautions the scholar against applying the knowledge he has obtained from other traditions to his own arena of research too quickly but at the same time it helps him recognize that he will have to do this eventually.

Step 6. Describing relationships and processes

After having named the phenomena, the phenomenologist then notes how they are interrelated and seeks to identify processes among them. Myths, for example, are often related to rituals; myths form the context for ritual activities and rituals bring myths into the present experience of believers. Another example is that art often depicts scriptural teaching and may offer a moral lesson. Processes can be seen, for example, when beliefs change to keep pace with scientific discoveries or when rituals take on new meanings within a community in the light of incursions from outside forces — such as occurred in Africa during the era of European colonization. A description of the phenomena of any religion, therefore, includes the relationships between various classifications of the phenomena and it incorporates processes such as change, development, crises, growth or stagnation.

By acknowledging the dynamic character of religious phenomena, the scholar avoids the error of simply comparing 'descriptive typologies' without considering how historical or cultural developments have influenced them. In her review of the history of phenomenology, Ursula King (1983, 88) adopts the term 'historical phenomenology' to define what I mean at this stage in the method. This term, she contends, 'is perhaps the most appropriate to describe a strongly historically grounded, but systematically and comparatively oriented study of religious phenomena'. As we noted earlier, Wilfred Cantwell Smith (1978, 156–7) calls this the 'cumulative tradition' by which he means the phenomena ('temples, scriptures, theological systems, dance patterns, legal and other social institutions, moral codes and so on') which are 'transmitted from one person, one generation to another'.

In this book, in addition to assigning names to the phenomena (myths, rituals, sacred practitioners, art, scripture, morality and beliefs), we shall consider the classifications in the light of their interrelationships and processes. This method will form the basis for our 'informed comparison' which we will apply to the paradigmatic model at the next step of the method.

It should be remembered, however, that noting relationships and processes, even more than naming or classifying the phenomena, requires the scholar to adopt an active role in the development of phenomenological descriptions. This is because relationships and processes emerge out of the interaction between the scholar and the religious data and are not simply part of the phenomena themselves. Sharpe (1986, 232) explains that 'a phenomenon . . . is given in the interplay and interpenetration of subject and object, in the very act of understanding'. The scholar's ability to note relations and processes among the phenomena, therefore, results from his creative interaction with his research data.

Step 7. Constructing the paradigmatic model

The scholar is now ready to draw a paradigm or a pattern for the study of any religion. Initially, the paradigm (as a universal model) enables the scholar to note similarities or describe differences among various traditions at any point within the classifications of the phenomena or their interrelationships and processes. For example, although the same types of beliefs are found in every religion, the model helps us see in what ways their content varies, how that content influences the adherent's experience of the sacred, and what types of rituals are emphasized to re-enforce those beliefs. We can also see how certain types of beliefs in one tradition may have been modified under historical, scientific or intellectual influences but how in another tradition they may have remained relatively unchanged.

This results in an understanding of the meaning of the classifications of religious phenomena in general. What the observer learned through his insight into the meaning of the phenomena of a specific tradition can be used to analyse similar phenomena derived from other traditions. Basic understandings of each category are built up through contrast and comparison so that we can speak, for example, of the religious significance of myths or rituals in general. Moreover, the description of the relationships between the phenomena and their processes are placed on to the paradigmatic model so that a broad view of these relationships and processes may be attained for all religions.

In a second, significant, way, moreover, the paradigm enables the scholar to develop a statement regarding the core concern or overriding principal characteristic of any specific religious tradition he is studying. For example, if a phenomenologist read the teachings attributed originally to the Buddha and then observed the activities occurring among Buddhist monks in Sri Lanka, he might conclude that the essential unifying factor among Theravada (Old School) Buddhism is the endeavour to become detached from all worldly concerns and enter into an unparalleled experience of peace and serenity. Each ritual of meditation, every teaching concerning morality, and the monk's vows of worldly renunciation, when seen in the light of the Buddha's dialogues, would re-enforce this interpretation.

The paradigmatic model, therefore, operates much like an architect's plan for the construction of a building. It enables the trained craftsman to see specific aspects within the design, the interrelation of these aspects and what the end product will be. The craftsman is able to view the plan in microscopic detail or to see the design as a whole. He could also compare the type of building envisaged in the architect's plan with other buildings of similar or differing construction and design. In the same way the student of religion studies specific phenomena within particular traditions, names these phenomena, notes their relationships and processes and perceives the broader meaning implied by observing them as a whole.

Step 8. Performing the eidetic intuition: Understanding the meaning of religion

After naming the phenomena, describing the relationships and processes among them and constructing the paradigmatic model, the eidetic intuition itself may occur, namely, the seeing into the essence or the meaning of religion. The eidetic intuition is different from defining religion since it occurs after the previous steps have been taken and results from interaction with the phenomena themselves. In Chapter One, we discussed definitions of religion and arrived, following Hall, Pilgrim and Cavanagh, at a working definition of religion. As a working definition is functional, we placed it at the beginning of the description of phenomenological research. The eidetic intuition may be called a substantive definition and is derived at the conclusion of phenomenological studies. Working definitions offer a direction for the research to proceed; the eidetic intuition reflects the results of that research.

The beginning and the end of the study of religion are, nevertheless, interrelated and thus to some degree any working or functional definition offers a preliminary direction which could potentially affect the outcome of research. Pettersson and Akerberg (1981, 61) call this one of the 'dilemmas' of the phenomenological method: 'A phenomenological research that does not have a certain idea of religion from the outset can never reach its true object — religion as *religion.*'

In Chapter One we also looked at the philosophical conception of the eidetic intuition suggested by Husserl. The notion of intuition as applied to religious phenomena needs further explication at this point. C. J. Bleeker (1963, 3) argued that intuition means 'vision', a search for or a seeing into 'the essentials of religious phenomena'. To accomplish this, he defined three essential enquiries: into the *theoria* of the phenomena; into the *logos* of the phenomena; and into the *entelecheia* of the phenomena.

For Bleeker, enquiry into the *theoria* of the phenomena meant to seek to understand 'the implications of the various aspects of religion which occur all over the world' (p. 16). Bleeker is here referring to what we called the naming of the phenomena (Step 5). The *logos* of the phenomena refers to a 'hidden structure' which operates according to 'strict inner laws' (p. 17). In other words, each religion possesses a logical order which when comprehended enables the scholar to understand its various components and how they interrelate. This seems to correspond to what we called the relationships and processes among the phenomena (Step 6) which can then be placed on to a paradigmatic model (Step 7).

By *entelecheia*, Bleeker was referring to a dynamic process. Religions are not static; hence the search for essentials will not produce rigid and timeless prescriptions of their meaning. Bleeker contended that 'the essence is realized by its manifestations' (p. 14). This means that the scholar must engage actively with the phenomena in order to perceive their essential meaning in their complex manifestations. By describing the phenomena, by noting their relationships and processes and by constructing the paradigm, the scholar is able to 'intuit' the essence of religion in the phenomena themselves. As Diogenes Allen (1985, 259) rightly observes, the term 'intuition' in this sense does not mean 'having an inspired idea' but literally 'looking at'. It is a comprehensive vision created out of the scholar's direct interaction with the data of religious experience which, again in Allen's words, serve as '*examples* or instances of the general essence' (p. 260).

Two phenomenologists who have sought to define the essence of religion include Mircea Eliade and W. Cantwell Smith. Eliade (1959) finds the meaning of religion in the dichotomy between the sacred and the profane. For religious people, both space and time are broken into by manifestations of the sacred (hierophanies). For example, when Jacob, in the biblical story (Gen. 28, 10–22), had a dream of a stairway reaching to heaven and angels walking up and down it, he interpreted the experience as revealing the sacred. He subsequently built an altar at Beth-el in response to this revelation — thus separating the space around the hierophany from all other space. The altar represented sacred ground, the place where the hierophany occurred, and all other space was orientated around it (Eliade, 1959, 26).

Eliade's eidetic intuition is portrayed in Figure 2.1. This diagram shows that profane space and time are invaded by hierophanies around which religious people define their existence through myths, rituals, sacred practitioners and the other phenomena of religion.

Wilfred Cantwell Smith (1978, 170–9) identifies the locus of religion in

Figure 2.1: ELIADE'S EIDETIC INTUITION

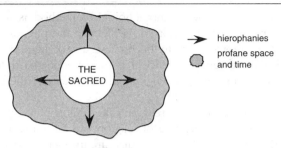

personal faith. He believes that each individual responds to a transcendent reality in an intensely personal way which can never be fully understood or objectively described. Nevertheless, personal faith occurs within the cumulative tradition and thus can be observed in its myths, rituals, beliefs, art, sacred practitioners and other phenomena. Individuals within the same cumulative tradition respond in personal faith to transcendence through shared phenomena and hence express their personal faith in a similar way. Figure 2.2 illustrates Smith's perception of the eidetic intuition.

Figure 2.2: SMITH'S PERCEPTION OF THE EIDETIC INTUITION

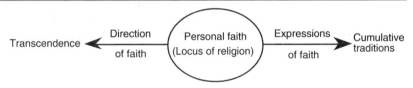

These brief descriptions of Eliade's and Smith's statements on the essence of religion show that an eidetic intuition seeks to decipher a universal meaning for religion based on comparative studies conducted among particular phenomena within specific traditions. As Douglas Allen notes (1978, 163–4), this does not reduce religious phenomena to some 'common denominator' but represents a process of 'integration' leading to understanding. By analysing many traditions and seeing into the essence of each, Eliade and Smith intuit patterns of meaning which they portray as being applicable to all religions. Moreover, they maintain the attitudinal phases within the process, described in Steps 1–3, by offering meanings which could be affirmed by adherents themselves.

Step 9. Testing the intuition

The final stage in the phenomenological method is to return to the phenomena, test the intuition in the light of the phenomena, and make revisions where necessary. In this process, any of the previous steps in the method may be retraced. Since it is the phenomena themselves which determine the meaning of religion, all statements of the eidetic intuition remain accountable to them.

The phenomenology of religion (like philosophical phenomenology) admits that no final meaning of religion can be apprehended. Religious studies, like any other human enquiry, are inexact, always in process, and hence never complete. It is precisely because the nature of religion includes intensely personal elements that the phenomenologist can only approximate its meaning, which makes it imperative, but difficult, to test his eidetic intuition.

In his book on the phenomenology of religion, M. Dhavamony (1973, 16) underscores the need for and the difficulty of completing this stage in the method. He claims that 'observations and experiment furnish us with evidence' from which we verify or falsify various hypotheses. Religious data, however, 'are objectively ascertainable but subjectively rooted facts' implying that phenomenological descriptions, structures and meanings are quite difficult to verify or to falsify.

Dhavamony, however, is merely pointing to a common problem in the study of religion which also occurs in all the human sciences. The process of achieving understanding and then of testing that understanding will always be, in Smart's words, 'crude' because the observer seeks to unravel a 'whole web of beliefs and resonances' (Smart, 1983, 270). The phenomenological test, however, is essential for the method since, in the

Table 2.1

SUMMARY OF THE PHENOMENOLOGICAL STEPS
IN THE STUDY OF RELIGION

1. Performing *epochē*.
2. Performing empathetic interpolation.
3. Maintaining *epochē*.
4. Describing the phenomena.
5. Naming the phenomena.
6. Decribing relationships and processes.
7. Constructing the paradigmatic model.
8. Performing the eidetic intuition.
9. Testing the intuition.

Figure 2.3: THE PHENOMENOLOGICAL METHOD

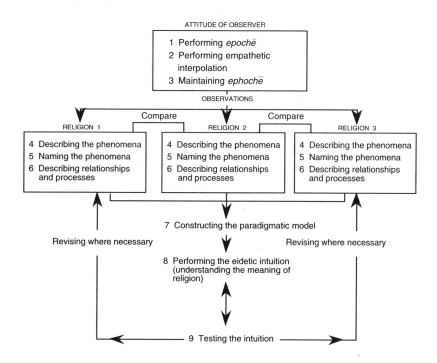

last analysis, the accuracy of the meanings proposed by various scholars depends on the phenomena.

Summary of the method

The phenomenology of religion, as we have described it including its inherent limitations, applies the nine steps discussed above (see the summary in Table 2.1) to the field of religion which we have defined based on Hall, Pilgrim and Cavanagh's working definition in the light of Ninian Smart's model of 'family resemblances'. Figure 2.3 illustrates the phenomenological steps using this working definition.

The distinction between the phenomenology and the history of religion

Some of the scholars I have cited above, such as W. Brede Kristensen and Mircea Eliade, have called themselves historians of religion rather than phenomenologists. As I have noted, methodological issues have determined the selection of these terms, and thus before concluding this chapter I must state the approach of this book towards the distinction between the phenomenology and the history of religion.

The Swedish historian George Widengren has insisted on maintaining this distinction, arguing that phenomenology describes and scientifically classifies the expressions of religion whereas history examines developments within various religions according to the specific method of historical analysis (cited by Sharpe, 1986, 242–43). Kristensen also maintained the distinction, although, like Widengren, he saw the two disciplines as being closely related. The phenomenologist, he contended, begins with specific data and then seeks to understand them among many religious traditions in order 'to gain an overall view of the ideas and motives which are of decisive importance in the History of Religion' (cited by Plantinga, 1989, 175).

This implies that the historian of religion describes the specific background to and developments within any particular religious tradition and leaves the task of comparing the phenomena of the various religions to the phenomenologist. Such comparisons, however, cannot be undertaken without reference to history, requiring the phenomenologist to work closely with the historian.

Eliade (1969, 9) adopts another approach by introducing the idea that the history of religions involves hermeneutics, that is, an interpretation of the meaning of religious data which attempts 'to show how these meanings have been experienced and lived in the various cultures and historical moments'. He denies that the value of the history of religions is simply to catalogue data. Its purpose rather is, by the use of the empirical method, to gain an 'understanding' of 'a religious experience or a religious conception of the world' (Eliade, 1959, 88).

What Eliade seems to be describing is what I have called the phenomenology of religion — including Step 6 which recognizes the historical processes operating within the various traditions and Step 8 on attaining the eidetic intuition. Discrepancies among scholars regarding the appropriate name for this method may result from the charge summarized by Ursula King (1983, 39) that phenomenology classifies data 'irrespective of any historical sequence' and thus is 'ahistorical if not to say anachronistic'.

If by phenomenology we mean merely producing descriptions from observations without understanding their relationships to other phenomena and processes within their cumulative traditions and then sterilely classifying the data in order to derive 'essences', King's objection would be legitimate. But what I mean by the phenomenology of religion corresponds to the working together of the historical and observational methods as advocated by the scholars I have mentioned such as Kristensen, Widengren, Bleeker, Eliade, Smith and Smart.

The phenomenology of religion as it is understood in this book, therefore, includes the history of religion and comparative data under the broad headings of *epochē* and eidetic intuition as specifically defined by the nine steps detailed above. It admits with Eliade (1969, 7) that 'there is no such thing as a "pure" religious datum, outside of history'. Moreover, it recognizes a certain tension between obtaining historical data and seeing into phenomenological essences, but following George Schmid (1979, 4), this book regards phenomenology as an 'integral science of religion' which seeks 'to find in the chaos of the many' a 'sort of order which binds the many into one'.

References

ALLEN, D.   1985   *Philosophy for Understanding Theology* (London, SCM Press).

ALLEN, D.   1978   *Structure and Creativity in Religion: Hermeneutics in Mircea Eliade's Phenomenology and New Directions* (The Hague, Mouton).

BLEEKER, C. J.   1963   *The Sacred Bridge: Researches into the Nature and Structure of Religion* (Leiden, Brill).

BLEEKER, C. J. 1971 'Comparing the religio-historical and the theological method', *Numen*, XVIII, 9–29.

DHAVAMONY, M.   1973   *Phenomenology of Religion* (Rome, Gregorian Univ. Press).

ELIADE, M.   1959   *The Sacred and the Profane*, trans. W. R. Trask (New York, Harcourt, Brace).

ELIADE, M.   1969   *The Quest: History and Meaning in Religion* (Chicago, Univ. of Chicago Press).

KING, U.   1983   'Historical and phenomenological approaches to the study of religion: Some major developments and issues under debate since 1950', in F. Whaling (ed.), *Contemporary Approaches to the Study of Religion: Volume I: The Humanities* (Berlin, Mouton), 29–164.

KRISTENSEN, W. B.   1969   'The meaning of religion', in J. D. Bettis (ed.), *Phenomenology of Religion* (New York, Harper and Row), 31–51.

PETTERSSON, O. and H. AKERBERG   1981   *Interpreting Religious Phenomena* (Stockholm, Almquist and Wiksell).

PLANTINGA, R. J.   1989   'W. B. Kristensen and the study of religion', *Numen*, XXXVI, 173–88.

PLATVOET, J. G.   1990   *Akan Traditional Religion: A Reader* (Harare, Univ. of Zimbabwe, Dept. of Religious Studies, Classics and Philosophy).

RUDOLPH, K.   1989   'Mircea Eliade and the "history" of religions', *Religion*, XIX, 101–27.

SCHMID, G.   1979   *Principles of an Integral Science of Religion*, trans. J. Wilson (The Hague, Mouton).

SHARPE, E   1971   *Fifty Key Words: Comparative Religion* (Richmond VA, John Knox Press).

SHARPE, E.   1986   *Comparative Religion: A History* (London, Duckworth).

SMART, N.   1973   *The Phenomenon of Religion* (New York, Seabury).

SMART, N.   1983   'The scientific study of religion in its plurality', in F. Whaling (ed.), *Contemporary Approaches to the Study of Religion: Volume I: The Humanities* (Berlin, Mouton), 365–78.

SMITH, W. C.   1972   *The Faith of Other Men* (San Francisco, Harper and Row).

SMITH, W. C.   1978   *The Meaning and End of Religion* (San Francisco, Harper and Row).

VAN DER LEEUW, G.   1938   *Religion in Essence and Manifestation* (London, Allen and Unwin).

WIEBE, D.   1981   *Religion and Truth: Towards an Alternative Paradigm for the Study of Religion* (The Hague, Mouton).

Questions and Activities

Questions for discussion

1. Identify similarities and differences between the concept of *epochē* as used in philosophy and as it is used in the phenomenology of religion.

2. Discuss the two terms 'empathy' and 'interpolate'. How do they work together to help the scholar 'get inside' a religion?

3. Is there a contradiction between refusing to comment on truth claims and the truth claims of a religion itself? If so, how would phenomenology attempt to overcome the contradiction?

4. Steps 4 through 7 in the phenomenological study of religion are interlinked. Describe how each leads to the other.

5. Why do words like 'witchcraft' and 'magic' distort the understanding of phenomena rather than describe them? Can you think of other examples?

6. What is meant by the eidetic intuition? Discuss either Eliade or Smith's diagram as offering a model for religious meaning.

Projects and activities

1. Attend a religious ceremony the beliefs of which you personally do not uphold. Suspend your judgements and empathize with the religion. List

the problems you encountered in this process.

2. Observe any religious ritual and then describe it. Note any words you use in your description which actually interpret rather than describe the ritual.

3. Use the paradigm drawn in this chapter with reference to any religion. Do the categories always fit?

Chapter Three
Why Did the Phenomenology of Religion Develop?

The phenomenological method in the study of religion emerged out of a larger movement which developed during the late nineteenth century which emphasized the scientific study of religion. Phenomenology accepted, along with other scientific approaches, the need to describe religion objectively. In this sense, it reacted against all forms of theological compartmentalization. We will return briefly to this point later. Phenomenology also reacted against three principal tendencies found historically within scientific approaches to religious studies: the explanation of religious phenomena exclusively in terms of disciplines other than religion itself such as sociology, psychology or anthropology (scientific reductionism); the evolutionary assumptions behind most theories concerning the origins of religion; and the projectionist explanations of religion.

Scientific reductionism

We have already encountered the problem of reductionism in the definitions of religion. Hall, Pilgrim and Cavanagh call reductionism a form of narrowness characterized by compartmentalization; Barnhart says it results in expansive definitions. Reductionism means to explain religious phenomena (hence, *reducing* it) in terms of the methods employed and the conclusions reached by disciplines other than religion. Rituals, for example, can be explained as fulfilling certain functions in society such as organizing the relationships between the sexes and between parents and children. Such functions, moreover, are often identified as root causes behind the development of religion as a human phenomenon.

The social sciences have shown a particular tendency towards reductionism. The Dutch scholar, J. G. Platvoet (1990, 20), contends that this has occurred because 'the primary field of the social sciences is not the religions themselves'. The psychologist, for example, tends to interpret religious phenomena in terms of emotional needs and may thus ignore the religious meanings of myths, rituals, sacred practitioners and other phenomena for believers.

The phenomenologist argues that explanations of religion in terms of other disciplines distort the phenomena *from the point of view of the believer* by forcing religious data to conform to the presuppositions of a particular discipline rather than allowing the phenomena to speak for themselves. The American scholar Robert Segal (1989, 312) contends that phenomenologists would be aware, for example, of the Freudian interpretations of religion (which I will describe shortly) but would 'argue that those interpretations are, by definition, of psychology *rather than* religion' and hence reductionistic. Segal, nevertheless, contends that scientists of religion must employ reductionistic interpretations since, in his view, to adopt the perspective of the believer requires the scholar to *endorse* the view of the believer (Segal, 1983, 101). Phenomenologists have suggested that Segal's view misunderstands the role of empathy (step 2 in the method) and completely overlooks the requirement of scholars to maintain *epoche* concerning the truth claims of any religion (step 3) (Cox, 1994, 3-31).

A particularly good example of scientific reductionism is found in a book by Rodney Stark and William Bainbridge (1985) to which we referred in Chapter One when defining religion. Stark and Bainbridge argue from a sociological perspective that all humans seek rewards and avoid what they perceive to be costs. In some societies the rewards are scarce but the costs are many. Moreover, the rewards are unevenly distributed. As a result, humans create 'compensators', based on the belief that 'a reward will be obtained in the distant future' or in a context like heaven 'which cannot be immediately verified' (p. 6).

For Stark and Bainbridge, therefore, religion operates within societies by providing compensators for the scarcity and unequal distribution of rewards. This explanation reduces religion to a sociological function, the establishment through beliefs, myths, rituals, laws and so on of compensating factors for deprivation.

This analysis is not necessarily wrong and it may add significantly to an understanding of the role of religion within society. But it distorts the religious experience of the believer and hence distorts the phenomena. No believer will agree that his religious faith exists *exclusively* in order to compensate in the future for the current maldistribution of rewards in society. To hold such a position would involve a denial of belief itself.

As we have noted, one of the leading phenomenologists earlier in this century was W. Brede Kristensen who held the Chair of Religion at Leiden University in Holland. Kristensen voiced a strong opposition to scientific reductionism and he advocated the need to enter into the religious experience of the believers. His famous declaration that believers are always right was based on the conviction, as Richard Plantinga (1989, 177) explains, that it is the believers' 'sole right to testify about their religion'. This 'sole right' acts to correct the imbalances which result from discussions of religion exclusively from the 'outside'.

Harold Turner (1981, 14) argues that the tendency to reduce religious experience to social scientific explanations has been particularly prevalent in Africa. This has occurred partly as a result of attitudes of Western superiority displayed in accounts by nineteenth-century explorers, ethnographers, and missionaries. Turner contends that these earlier distortions of African religions will not be overcome if the social and behavioural sciences view African religions exclusively as objects for study, because the impression will be created 'that African religions are no more than social and psychological phenomena rather than essentially religious and worthy to be professed as the faith of persons'.

To omit those dimensions of the activities of any people which under our working definition would qualify as religious, therefore, is to distort the phenomena themselves. The tendency of many of the social sciences to do this explains the first fundamental reason why the phenomenological method for the study of religion was developed.

Evolutionary theories concerning the origin of religion

Explanations from other disciplines, as Preus (1989, 328) has noted, often search for the causes of religion in human societies. Historically, these were explained in terms borrowed from the theory of biological evolution as expounded by the nineteenth-century scientist, Charles Darwin, who posited that lower forms of life evolve into higher ones according to various processes inherent within nature. One of the best contemporary definitions of the theory of biological evolution is found in John Allegro's book, *Lost Gods* (1977, 10).

> For more than half of its existence, this planet was in no condition to support life. Then, about two thousand million years ago, a combination of climatic and environmental circumstances allowed the formation of a new and wonderful molecular structure that was able not only to reproduce itself, but to store and pass on to its offspring a chemical blueprint that determined its nature and function. Self-regenerating and self-duplicating life had been born. However, since no copying device in nature is entirely exact, once every so often the transmitted code varies slightly from its pattern. The result is a mutation, making the progeny in some way different from its parents. The change might be for the good, perhaps helping the offspring to adapt more readily to a change in environment, or for worse, depriving it of some faculty and thus threatening the strain with extinction. If the new organism is a success, it will proliferate at the expense of less-favoured neighbours, and its novel advantageous features will be transmitted by the revised blueprint for subsequent generations.

With the widespread acceptance of this theory as scientific fact, scholars began to look for parallel developments occurring in cultures, societies and religions. It was assumed that the universal religious tendency in humanity originated in a primitive form and gradually evolved into higher, more advanced expressions. This process is defined clearly by the Welsh scholar, Islwyn Blythin (1988, 10).

> With the influence of Darwin's theory of evolution extending beyond the boundaries of biology, the search for the essence of religion and the search for the origin of religion coincided. Man's religion, like his body, was thought to have evolved from inferior to more advanced forms, and there appeared a great interest in primitive religions which were held to contain the earliest aspirations of mankind.

We cannot include here samples from every scholar who adopted evolutionary assumptions for the study of religion, but brief summaries of some of the most influential theories are listed below.

Auguste Comte (1798–1857) Platvoet (1990, 14) calls Comte 'the father of sociology'. He is best known for his evolutionary thesis which suggests that humans pass through three stages in their mental development: from the theological through the metaphysical to the scientific. The theological stage is the earliest and most primitive in which humans conceive the forces of nature as persons they call gods. This is evident even in monotheistic types of religion which describe the ultimate form of nature as a supernatural being. The metaphysical stage represents a transition whereby the personified gods are replaced by abstract concepts and universal ideas. The final stage is that of positive science in which nature is understood not in terms of personal beings or abstract ideas but through empirical, verifiable and objective laws (Preus, 1987, 109–19).

Sir James Frazer (1854–1941) Like Comte, Frazer based his explanation of religion on human historical development in stages. For Frazer, however, the first stage was an age of magic through which humans sought to control or manipulate the forces of nature to attain certain desirable purposes. Religion developed as it became clear that nature did not always respond to magical incantations or formulae. Religion, therefore, developed as humans appealed to a force or forces outside themselves to act in their own best interests.

Frazer argued that magic consistently failed to produce the successful manipulation of nature (false causation) and hence gave way to religion which characteristically seeks to appease the gods to achieve desired ends. Within religion, moreover, the observer can note developmental trends. In his discussion of the religious significance of trees, for example, Frazer (1923, 117) described how higher forms of religion develop from more primitive sources.

> Instead of regarding each tree as a living and conscious being, man now sees in it merely a lifeless, inert mass, tenanted for a larger or shorter time

by a supernatural being who, as he can pass freely from tree to tree, thereby enjoys a certain right of possession or lordship over trees, and, ceasing to be a tree-soul, becomes a forest-god.

Like Comte, Frazer saw the final stage of evolution as science, the empirical testing and verification of real causes and real effects according to the consistent laws of nature (Hutchison, 1969, 32–3).

E. B. Tylor (1832–1917) Tylor is famous for his influential theory of animism which traced the origin of religion to 'primitive man's' naïve tendency to perceive living souls (*anima*) in all forms of nature. We have already seen that Tylor defined religion as belief in spiritual or supernatural beings. This belief, for Tylor, originated in dreams. In his dream-life, a person is able to travel, talk to the living and the dead, or undergo experiences even while his body remains inert. Likewise, when a person dies, his body ceases to function but its life-giving power, the soul, continues to exist (1965, 16).

If humans have souls, by extension 'primitive man' supposed that all objects in nature must have souls. Trees, stones, animals, mountains and every other natural object possess a life-force. This led to polytheism which perceived powerful souls in objects and in non-physical spiritual forces. Later, some souls were conceived as being more powerful than others — giving rise to the idea of a sky god and eventually to monotheism, the highest form of religion (Preus, 1987, 139–42).

R. R. Marett (1866–1943) Marett was influenced initially by the writings of Bishop R. H. Codrington, a missionary to Melanesia, a group of islands in the West Pacific. Codrington had described the Melanesian belief in an impersonal force or mysterious power which the Melanesians called *mana* (Tokarev, 1989, 39–42). This force, because it was impersonal, could not be an object towards which people made direct appeals. Rather, either it was with a person conferring skills required to achieve desired ends (such as success in hunting) or it abandoned a person (thus explaining failures and misfortunes). Although *mana* could not be appealed to, it seemed to operate like a law explaining why the Melanesians created strict rules called *taboos* which the people were required to follow. Observance of the rules maintained the positive influence of *mana* whereas breaking them resulted in misfortune (Hutchison, 1969, 32).

Marett argued that the impersonal force observed by Codrington among the indigenous people of Melanesia referred to a general primitive belief which had developed prior to animism in human evolution. Marett called this impersonal force *pre-animism* or *dynamism*. Primitive people experienced fear, respect and wonder at the awesome power displayed in nature such as is visible in violent storms. This feeling of awe at the impersonal power of nature, or what Sharpe (1986, 67) describes as the 'uncanny', explained for Marett the roots of religion. It was not until later that humans personified this power first in what Tylor called animism and later by creating gods and finally God (Platvoet, 1990, 16–17).

Wilhelm Schmidt (1868–1954) Schmidt was a Roman Catholic missionary who held the idea that the original religion of primitive society was monotheism or belief in one High God. Although he distinguished his position from earlier evolutionary theories, Schmidt's view can be regarded as a kind of evolutionary process in reverse. Primitive beliefs do not begin in lower forms and move to higher ones; rather, the early belief in a High God degenerated over time, as Platvoet notes, into forms of 'naturism, fetishism, ghost-worship, animism, totemism or magism' (p. 27).

Schmidt explained this process by arguing that the High God among the primitives often is described in myths as withdrawing from day-to-day life to the remote regions of the sky. The most common concerns of people, therefore, were relinquished to lesser deities, ancestors and other spiritual beings. This produced polytheism. The great later monotheistic religions have developed out of these lower forms and may be regarded as recovering the original primal vision of belief in one God (Eliade, 1969, 23–5).

The theories noted above all share preconceived ideas about development. They begin with evolutionary assumptions and impose them on the religious data. Phenomenologists accused the scholars who propounded these theories of having interpreted the phenomena before actually observing them (Kristensen, 1969, 48). Beginning with the application of Darwin's biological theory to religion, they moulded the data of religion to fit their evolutionary presuppositions.

Phenomenologists adopted the procedure of *epochē* to avoid this error. The suspension of judgement intends that the data of religious experience speak for themselves and that the resulting descriptions provide the source for any theories regarding the meaning of religion within human life.

Projectionist theories

Projectionist theories assume that religion has developed out of some human need which has been enlarged or projected on to an ultimate being. All forms of the projectionist hypothesis, therefore, contend that God is created in the image of man rather than man being created in the image of God.

One of the earliest and most influential exponents of this view was the nineteenth-century philosopher Ludwig Feuerbach (1804–1872). Feuerbach ([1854] 1975, 115–28) believed that humans are aware of their own finite situation but long for the infinite. They are familiar with their own imperfections, but seek perfection. They recognize their own restricted knowledge, but want to know everything. They experience powerlessness, but want to become omnipotent. They fail in love, peace and justice, but seek to achieve these ideals.

Out of their own finitude, imperfections, limited knowledge, powerlessness and injustice, therefore, humans have 'projected' an ideal on to a creature of their own making they call God. God is infinite, perfect, all-knowing, all-powerful, all-loving and the king of justice.

But where do these qualities or ideas of infinity, perfection, knowledge, power, love and justice originate? Clearly, they are human ideas resulting from the desire within humanity to achieve them completely. But since humans cannot achieve them completely, they invent the all-perfect Being and project these very human qualities on to this Being. This is what is meant by the statement that God is created in the image of Man.

This process is called by Feuerbach the anthropomorphizing of God or defining God by human characteristics (p. 118). Feuerbach argued that this actually harms humanity and prevents people from achieving their real potential. It alienates each person from his inner self and thus from his own best qualities. Instead of seeking perfection outside themselves, therefore, humans should seek to perfect their own inner selves and their societies.

For Feuerbach, therefore, the projection of human qualities on to some transcendent object prevents humanity from achieving its ideal. What is needed is a reversal of the subject and the predicate. Instead of saying, 'God is love', we must say, 'Love is god'. Rather than affirming, 'God is all-knowing', we should say, 'Knowledge is god'. God must not be the subject of the sentence but the predicate; humans will then to able to foster the very best qualities they already recognize within themselves (Küng, 1981, 200–2).

Feuerbach's projectionist idea has influenced the study of religion in many disciplines. E. B. Tylor's theory of animism, for example, is based not only on evolutionary theory but also on the idea that humans project spiritual beings out of their own dream-life on to all objects in nature. Pettersson and Akerberg (1981, 97) go so far as to claim that 'Tylor's theory is a completely psychological interpretation'. This is true also of Marett's concept of dynamism which likewise results from a presupposition of psychic projection. According to Marett, the primitive's belief in a dynamic and mysterious impersonal force influencing all things has resulted from his sense of awe, mystery and wonder in response to the power of nature.

Although the projectionist idea has been and still continues to influence religious studies, we will look here at two classic proponents of this theory. Sigmund Freud, in the field of psychology, and Emile Durkheim, from a sociological perspective, both adopted it in their analyses of the role of religion within human life.

Sigmund Freud (1865–1939) Freud, who founded the modern science of psychoanalysis, wrote widely in the field of religion. One of his earliest contributions ([1913] 1945) concerned the origin of totemic symbols among primitive societies and their relationship to taboos. He discovered a universal primitive prohibition against incest and suggested that originally a primeval horde of male sons killed their father because they were jealous of his relationship with their mother (the Oedipus complex). This produced guilt and resulted first in totemic animals acting as a substitute for the murdered father (hence, a prohibition against eating the totem) and second in the restriction against incest in reaction to the original sexual advances of the sons toward their mother.

Although Freud's theories regarding totemism and taboos resulted from an interpretation of psychological projections of perceived primitive impulses within humanity, this idea is largely discredited today. His continuing impact on the study of religion, however, comes from a different application of the projection theory which explains religion as resulting from the human needs for comfort against perceived threats, authority in moral action, and answers to ultimate questions (Freud, 1964, 162).

A recurring theme in all religion is the problem of human suffering. Freud believed that this produced the need for comfort evidenced in the religious belief that all pain will cease in a future life. Moreover, death, which is the greatest human fear, is stripped of its power by religion's promise of eternal life. This promise corresponds to a parent's response to a frightened child who awakes at night and is afraid of the dark. The parent comforts the child by turning on the light and announcing, 'There is nothing to be afraid of; everything is all right.' This is precisely what religion does when, in Freud's words, it teaches that 'over each one of us there watches a benevolent Providence' (1961, 19). This Providence is projected out of the human need for comfort in the face of life's misfortunes.

Religion also authoritatively provides moral rules for its adherents to obey. If these precepts are followed, rewards result; if they are disregarded, calamity occurs. The need for moral laws, just like the need for comfort, has its roots in childhood experience. The same parent who took care of the child and kept him safe from danger taught him about right and wrong behaviour. When the child obeyed, the parent rewarded him. When he broke the rules, he was punished. For Freud, this childhood experience is projected on to moral codes and persists as religion.

A third function of religion is to provide answers about the nature of reality itself. Although this aspect of religion most closely resembles philosophy and science, religion continues to project childhood needs by looking for answers which can be given from outside and which come with absolute authority. The parent is regarded by a child as an all-knowing source of information about the world. God is the projected parent who 'reveals' truth to the believers in a way far different from philosophy with its emphasis on reason and science through its method of empirical investigation.

Religion for Freud is a neurosis, a psychological malady, because it keeps its adherents permanently fixed in a state of childish illusion rather than allowing them to grow up into mature adults who face life realistically. Healthy adults realize that their parents could not really remove all dangers from life, that they could not dictate moral laws and that they were not infallible sources of knowledge. Any adult who still regards his parents as he did as a child can rightly be regarded as psychologically disturbed. Religion, however, projects just these infantile illusions on to the being of God and thus prevents people from responding to the real dangers and limitations within life in a psychologically healthy way.

Emile Durkheim (1858–1917) Platvoet calls the scholar Emile Durkheim 'the most important French sociologist after Comte' (1990, 17). Whereas Freud used Feuerbach's projection theory to explain the religious response psychologically, Durkheim applied the idea in a social context.

Durkheim begins by making a distinction (later expounded and re-interpreted by Mircea Eliade) between the sacred and the profane. Durkheim claims that this fundamental division 'is characteristic of all cultures' and that it 'divides the universe into exclusive departments' ([1915] 1976, 167). The sacred is expressed in any tradition by a 'collective consciousness' which is a fusion of individual and social consciousness. The collective consciousness impresses on the individual rules of respect by making him identify completely with the society and thus connecting him with something greater than himself. By contrast, the profane centres on 'personal preoccupations', 'private existence' and 'egoistic concerns'.

The sacred, therefore, is found in the society; the profane in the merely private and individual. This distinction informs Durkheim's functional understanding of religious beliefs and practices as uniting 'into one single moral community called a church all those who adhere to them' (p. 47).

The most elementary form of religious life (following the title of Durkheim's classic book) can be seen in primitive societies where the sacred is identified clearly with the clan and its totemic symbol. A clan is the basic social organization of primitive people and a totem is an animal or sometimes a plant or vegetable which represents or symbolizes the clan. The totem is what Durkheim variously calls the clan's 'emblem', 'ensign' or 'crest' (p. 113).

The clan is united by its sharing of this common emblem. It is not a family in the sense that it does not consist of blood relations nor do its members necessarily live in the same location. The clan shares the same rules of respect, follows the same rituals, and thus participates in what

Durkheim calls the same 'totemic cult'. The totem attains its sacred power, particularly when the clan comes together or assembles (Preus, 1987, 173–4).

Although the totem is regarded by the believers as sacred, it actually stands as the emblem of the clan suggesting that the clan is sacred. The clan, however, is actually a social organization consisting of various rules, customs, practices, beliefs and order. Society, therefore, is sacred; society is God. The totem, as the objectification of the clan, is venerated and thus the clan actually worships itself. As an object of worship, society obtains god-like or transcendent power by determining for its members, in Platvoet's words, 'their thought, perceptions, behaviour, and activities' (1990, 17).

In Durkheim's analysis, the object of worship results from a societal projection. Society needs to bind its members together, to create a sense of loyalty, to enforce rules of behaviour and to preserve its values. By projecting itself on to a divine or supernatural reality, society attains absolute power over its members and makes the collective consciousness sacred.

Both Freud and Durkheim follow Feuerbach by locating the source of religion in a human projection which arises out of either individual or social needs. The phenomenological approach to religion initially accuses such theories, just as it did other scientific approaches, of reducing religion to just one aspect of human life. In Freud's case, religion is reduced to infantile desires; in Durkheim, to a social function.

Projectionist theories, however, do more than reduce religion to other disciplines. They actually comment on the state of ultimate reality. Feuerbach's atheism is reflected in Freud's judgement on the illusory nature of religion and in Durkheim's claim that society is its own divine being. Projectionist theories, therefore, begin with the assumption that no transcendent object of religious faith actually exists. As a result, their analysis of the meaning of religion is explained exclusively in terms of human needs.

In reaction to this, the phenomenology of religion asserts that statements about reality distort religious phenomena because they treat religion as something which can be separated from the perspective of the believing community. The stages of empathetic interpolation and maintaining *epoche* ensure that the phenomenologist makes every effort to enter into the experience of the adherents while refusing to make any statements at all about the believers' truth claims. Failure to observe these principles, according the phenomenological method, impedes the scholar from achieving an understanding of religious traditions.

Theological reductionism

So far we have discussed the reaction from within the phenomenology of religion to reductionist, evolutionary and projectionist interpretations of religious data. Another form of reductionism against which phenomenology reacts is the theological, in which every religion is evaluated according to the criteria established by one alone. Religions which emphasize that their beliefs are revealed by God often interpret every other religion in the light of that claim. Antonio Barbose da Silva (1982, 73) calls this a theologically normative approach where 'its proponent takes one religion as the only "true religion" (which is usually his own), and compares it with all other religions regarded as false ones'.

Christians, for example, have struggled with this issue particularly since the expansion of Protestant missions in the nineteenth and twentieth centuries into Asia, Africa and other parts of the so-called 'non-Christian' world. Many nineteenth-century missionaries also accepted some of the scientific approaches, particularly the evolutionary thesis, but used them to interpret Christianity as the highest form of religion. This added a theological dimension to the theories of evolutionary exponents such as Comte, Tylor and Marett.

A good example of the use of a scientific approach for theological purposes is found in the *Report of Commission IV* on the Missionary Message following the Edinburgh World Missionary Conference of 1910. The *Report* was compiled by the Scottish theologian D. S. Cairns who devoted a section of it to Tylor's classification of 'animistic religions' applied in an evolutionary context. Cairns writes, for example: 'Among the animistic tribes there is manifested in some cases a rudimentary moral sense and a dim consciousness of sin' (World Missionary Conference, 1910, 27). The assumption behind this judgement is that Christianity possesses a high moral sense and a full consciousness of sin which can be awakened in its primitive form among animistic peoples.

Moreover, the *Report of Commission IV* claims that the monotheism of Christianity appeals greatly to animists. Cairns demonstrates again his evolutionary assumptions when he observes 'it may seem strange that truths which to us are so elementary, as the unity and omnipotence of God, should come home with such kindling power to the hearts of men'. After reading the responses of many missionaries from Africa, Cairns concludes that 'the whole life of the animist . . . lies under the incubus of terror' (p. 219).

The *Report of Commission IV* provides an example of reductionism where a theological belief (in this case the supremacy of Christianity) is interpreted in terms of pre-conceived scientific theories (animism and evolution). It therefore doubly distorts the phenomena of religion because it imposes both personal and academic presuppositions *and* makes claims about the nature of ultimate reality.

The phenomenological objection, however, is not against theology but against theological interpretations of religion in the light of certain truth claims. The theological approach fails to describe or appreciate religious expressions of those who are not believers in the so-called 'true' religion and, therefore, it blocks understanding.

Paradoxically, projectionist theories which make atheistic assumptions about reality may also be accused of theological reductionism. By making statements about the truth or falsehood of religious beliefs, they evaluate all truth claims in the light of their understanding of what is the ultimate. Feuerbach's reversal of the subject and predicate (not God is love, but love is God), therefore, represents a form of theological reductionism and is open to the same objections from a phenomenological perspective as those religions which claim to possess the only true, final or most perfect revelation from God.

The relationship of phenomenology to other ways of studying religion

Many students may conclude from this chapter that phenomenology opposes the study of religion from the perspectives of other disciplines such as sociology, anthropology and psychology or from the standpoints of philosophy or theology. Phenomenology, however, does not seek to discredit the significance nor the important contribution to knowledge which results from the study of religion from within various disciplines. In fact, these disciplines provide what Harold Turner (1981, 1–15) calls 'the milieu' into which religion is interwoven. But what they cannot do is to explain fully the meaning of religion because their object of concern is not the religious phenomena themselves but the application of their own disciplines to the religious phenomena. Phenomenology, Turner contends, is the study 'of *what* is interwoven into the milieu'. The proper subject matter of the phenomenologist is the religious phenomena and hence phenomenology affirms religion as a discipline *sui generis*, as a classification of its own.

The claim that the study of religion comprises a field unique to itself and hence is irreducible to other disciplines has created a great deal of controversy among scholars. For example, Ivan Strenski of the University of California at Santa Barbara accuses phenomenologists on this point of fearing 'the loss of the precious epistemological privileges which they awarded themselves' (1993, 5). Strenski calls for an interdisciplinary approach to religious studies arguing that 'good understanding demands knowledge in context - *in relation*' (p. 1).

Turner acknowledges this clearly by insisting that religion cannot be understood outside of its context, but only in relation to its milieu. The endeavour to stake out a ground for the study of religion as religion, however, as we have seen in this chapter, was undertaken by phenomenologists for clear methodological reasons, the chief consideration being the attempt to understand religion from the 'inside' using the techniques of *epoche* and empathetic interpolation. This method, which aims at achieving an empirically testable interpretation of the meaning of religion (the eidetic intuition) becomes fully interdisciplinary when religious meanings are employed alongside explanations emanating from other disciplines such as sociology or psychology.

Students also often confuse the objection of phenomenology to projectionist theories as a defence for the belief in God. *Phenomenology does not defend the belief in God nor attack the belief in God.* It affirms that believers within many religious traditions remain loyal to what they conceive to be God. The phenomenologist, in search of understanding, empathizes with that loyalty without making any judgement on the object of religious faith. This approach clearly distinguishes phenomenology from theology, which presumes that the sacred actually exists and has manifested itself in ways described within the various traditions.

Figure 3.1:   WAYS OF STUDYING RELIGION

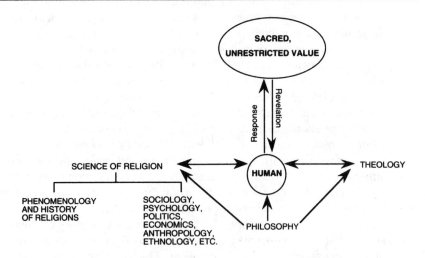

Figure 3.1, which is adapted from the work of Harold Turner (McKenzie, 1990, 29–33), is presented here to clarify the relationship between the phenomenological method and other ways of studying religion. It places phenomenology within the scientific study of religion but distinguishes it from other sciences as a method for studying religion from within and as a discipline in its own right. The diagram also includes philosophy as an

approach to studying the relationship between the human and the sacred using the tools of linguistic analysis, methods of knowing and logic. A legitimate place for theology is reserved as a method for studying what any specific religion perceives to be the revelation of the divine to the human. Because of their particular approaches, however, neither philosophy nor theology should be classified among the sciences of religion, although they are related to them by their common interest in the sacred–human relationship.

Summary and points of clarification

In this chapter we have seen that the phenomenology of religion developed as a reaction against scientific and theological reductionism, evolutionary assumptions about the origin of religion and projectionist theories about the nature of reality. The phenomenological *objections* are summarized in the following points.

Reductionism   Religion is explained in non-religious categories.

Presuppositions The religious phenomena are explained prior to actual observations in order to fit preconceived theories.

Distortion   The phenomena are distorted from the point of view of the believer.

Bias   Judgements are made on the truth claims of the believers.

Lack of   Understanding of specific religious traditions and of
understanding religion in general is blocked.

The primary phenomenological *resolutions* to these objections are shown below.

The value of   Developing religious studies as a discipline in its own
religious studies right.

Epochē   As far as possible, suspending the observer's pre-conceived personal or academic judgements.

Empathetic   Entering into the life, practice and perspectives of
interpolation believers.

Maintaining   Avoiding verdicts concerning the truth claims of
epochē   adherents.

Eidetic intuition   Attaining understanding by seeing into the meaning of
religion.

It should be remembered that the objections noted above describe
general types of approaches and hence are characterizations by definition.
In reality, few scholars could be said to employ all the techniques against
which the phenomenologist objected. For example, E. B. Tylor (1891, 4–10)
who, as we have noted, has been widely criticized for his approach to the
study of so-called 'primitive religions', argued for a scientific approach to
the study of cultures by classifying data, comparing facts and ridding the
accounts of extraneous material. We also see this attitude in J. G. Frazer,
who in his preface to the abridged version of *The Golden Bough* (1923, vii),
acknowledged the limitations of his own explanation of religion by admitting
that he would 'always be ready to abandon it if a better can be suggested'.
The phenomenological objections listed above, therefore, represent
tendencies among certain scholars and disciplines but should not be applied
without qualification.

It should be stressed also that the reductionist, evolutionary and
projectionist assumptions outlined in this chapter have influenced the study
of religion historically but that many changes within the various disciplines,
including phenomenology, have occurred. Not every human science wants
or needs to explain religion strictly in narrow disciplinary terms. Moreover,
psychology and sociology should not be classified necessarily as projectionist
simply because Freud and Durkheim employed such an approach. Neither
should all theological methods be dismissed as reductionist. Many theological
approaches to religion seek to understand how humans have responded
differently to one transcendent reality.

In addition, the phenomenological resolutions should be understood in
the light of their own limitations. Religious studies, as Turner has noted, can
never be regarded as a discipline which operates in isolation from other
aspects within the human environment. In addition, as we have seen
earlier, *epochē* cannot be performed perfectly, empathetic interpolation is
prone to misunderstanding, maintaining *epochē* may distort the phenomena
from a believer's point of view, and the eidetic intuition never offers a final
or complete understanding of religion.

The phenomenological objections and their resolutions have been
sharply contrasted in this chapter in order to achieve clarity and to
demonstrate the historical background against which the phenomenological method developed. In studying and applying these distinctions,
the student should nonetheless recognize that the objections, because
they are characterizations, are overstated and that the resolutions contain
inherent problems of their own.

References

ALLEGRO, J. 1977 *Lost Gods* (London, Joseph).

BLYTHIN, I. 1986 *Religion and Methodology: Past and Present* (Swansea, Ty John Penry).

COX, J.L. 1994 'Religious studies by the religious: A discussion of the relationship between theology and the science of religion', *Journal for the Study of Religion*, VII (2), 3-31.

DA SILVA, A. B. 1982 *The Phenomenology of Religion as a Philosophical Problem* (Gleerup, CWK).

DURKHEIM, E. [1915] 1976 *The Elementary Forms of Religious Life*, trans. J. W. Swain (London, Allen and Unwin).

ELIADE, M. 1969 *The Quest: History and Meaning in Religion* (Chicago, Univ. of Chicago Press).

FEUERBACH, L. [1854] 1975 'Religion as a projection of human nature', in A. Frazier (ed.), *Issues in Religion: A Book of Readings* (New York, Van Nostrand), 115–28.

FRAZER, J. G. 1923 *The Golden Bough: A Study in Magic and Religion* (London, Macmillan).

FREUD, S. [1913] 1945 *Totem and Taboo: Resemblances Between the Psychic Lives of Savages and Neurotics*, trans. A. A. Brill (New York, Vintage Books).

FREUD, S. 1961 'The future of an illusion', in *The Standard Edition of the Complete Psychological Works of Sigmund Freud: Volume XXI (1927–1931)*, trans. J. Strachey (London, Hogarth), 5–56.

FREUD, S. 1964 'The question of a *weltanschauung*', in *The Standard Edition of the Complete Psychological Works of Sigmund Freud: Volume XXII (1932–1936)*, trans. J. Strachey (London, Hogarth), 158–86.

HUTCHISON, J. A. 1969 *Paths of Faith* (New York, McGraw-Hill).

KRISTENSEN, W. B. 1969 'The meaning of religion', in J. D. Bettis (ed.), *Phenomenology of Religion* (New York, Harper and Row), 31–51.

KÜNG, H. 1981 *Does God Exist?*, trans. E. Quinn (New York, Vintage Books).

MCKENZIE, P. R. 1990 'Phenomenology and "The Centre": The Leicester years', in A. F. Walls and W. R. Shenk (eds.), *Exploring New Religious Movements* (Elkhart IN, Mission Focus Publications), 29–33.

PLANTINGA, R. J. 1989 'W. B. Kristensen and the study of religion', *Numen*, XXXVI, 173–88.

PLATVOET, J. G. 1990 *Akan Traditional Religion: A Reader* (Harare, Univ. of Zimbabwe, Dept of Religious Studies, Classics and Philosophy).

PREUS, J. S.   1987   *Explaining Religion: Criticism and Theory from Bodin to Freud* (New Haven, Yale Univ. Press).

PREUS, J. S.   1989   'Explaining religion: Author's response' *Religion*, XIX, 324–9.

SEGAL, R.   1983   'In defense of reductionism', *Journal of the American Academy of Religion*, 51 (1), 97-124.

SEGAL, R.   1989   'Religionist and social scientific strategies', *Religion*, XIX, 310–16.

STARK, R. and BAINBRIDGE, W.   1985   *The Future of Religion: Secularization, Revival and Cult* (Berkeley and Los Angeles, Univ. of California Press).

STRENSKI, I.   1993   *Religion in Relation: Method, Application and Moral Location* (London, Macmillan).

TOKAREV, S.   1989   *History of Religion* (Moscow, Progress).

TURNER, H.   1981   'The way forward in the religious study of African primal religions', *Journal of Religion in Africa*, XII, 1–15.

TYLOR, E. B.   1891   *Primitive Culture* (London, John Murray).

TYLOR, E. B.   1965   'Animism', in W. Lessa and E. Vogt (eds.), *Reader in Comparative Religion: An Anthropological Approach* (New York, Harper and Row), 10–21.

WORLD MISSIONARY CONFERENCE   1910   *Report of Commission IV: The Missionary Message in Relation to Non-Christian Religions* (Edinburgh, Oliphant, Anderson and Ferrier).

Questions and Activities

Questions for discussion

1. Briefly define biological evolution. How is it applied to theories of the origin of religion?

2. Write brief summaries of the thought of one scholar who reduced religion to another discipline, one who adopted an evolutionary theory of the origin of religion, and one who presented a projectionist position. Compare your summaries. Can the work of any scholar fit into more than one category? Why or why not?

3. Describe the principal phenomenological objections to scientific reductionism, evolutionary ideas and projectionist theories.

4. Explain the following statement: 'Sigmund Freud's interpretation of religion may be correct scientifically, but it is wrong phenomenologically'.

5. What is theological reductionism? In the light of your answer, justify a legitimate place for theology in the study of the divine–human relationship. How does theology differ from phenomenology?

Projects and activities

1. By consulting basic books in anthropology, design a chart showing simply how evolutionary theory suggests that life evolved on earth. Using your imagination, attempt to design another chart which depicts religious evolution. Indicate which of the current religious traditions would represent the most primitive and which the most advanced. What problems do you encounter in this exercise?

2. Make an appointment with a lecturer in the psychology department. Design a simple questionnaire in which you include such questions as:
   a) Why do people believe in God?
   b) What function do you think religion plays in human emotions?
   c) Is it possible to be psychologically healthy and a firm adherent of a religion? Compile your results and compare them with the Freudian interpretation.

3. Obtain a Christian prayer book such as the Anglican *Book of Common Prayer*. Consult a prayer of confession. Analyse it for a) psychological desires for comfort, authority and answers; b) evidence that religion enforces social rules. Then, write a short essay (one page) on how a believer might experience the prayer. Compare this with your other analyses.

Chapter Four
The Phenomenological Method: A Case Study

In order to see how the phenomenological method can be applied, we now look at a case study extracted from a BA Honours thesis submitted to the University of Zimbabwe in Harare (Zhuwawo, 1990). The student, the late Revd Collen Zhuwawo, conducted research on a particular death ritual (*kurova guva*) among a Shona-speaking people called the Vashawasha living in a region approximately twenty kilometres north of Harare. Although Zhuwawo's descriptions form a composite of what generally occurs in the ritual, he based his results on field observations and interviews. In this case study, we will follow the phenomenological method to Step 5 and then examine how the method can be used to derive the meaning of specific types of phenomena, their structure and their essences.

The *kurova guva* ceremony

The background

The Vashawasha people are a sub-group of the Shona-speaking people called the Zezuru who now occupy a region in the north-central part of Zimbabwe surrounding Harare. M. F. C. Bourdillon (1987, 17) reports that the Zezuru group have resulted 'from numerous migrations' but, although they share a common language and culture with other Shona-speaking groups, they 'do not have a common history'.

The Shona themselves are believed to have originated from a series of migrations of Bantu ethnic groups who, according to Bourdillon (p. 7), arrived in Zimbabwe as early as the second century CE (Common Era) and eventually occupied most of the region between the Limpopo River, the Zambezi River, the Kalahari Desert and the mountains which today form the border between Mozambique and Zimbabwe. There is little agreement as to where the Shona actually came from (Samkange, 1968, 3), but many Shona groups refer to migrations from an unidentified place called *Guruwuskwa* (meaning 'big grass'). Zhuwawo reports that the Vashawasha people arrived in their present location in the early eighteenth century having migrated from the south near the present-day town of Masvingo.

The Vashawasha share many beliefs with other African peoples, including the central place of ancestors in religious life. In his classic book on African religions, E. G. Parrinder (1981, 24) claims that 'all Africans believe in the ancestors' who 'are regarded as having powers which are useful to men'. This belief is seen clearly in Zhuwawo's description of the *kurova guva* ceremony which, although forming a part of a larger series of death rituals, specifically aims at bringing the deceased home from wandering in the forest by ritually making him an ancestor who can employ his influence for the benefit of his family.

Since the Shona constitute a patrilineal society, the ritual is normally conducted for a man who has children, who has lived what the community regards as a morally upright life, and who has died what is considered a natural death (due to illness, for example, and not as a result of suicide) (Bourdillon, 1987, 209; see also Kileff and Kileff, 1988, 65). My own research among the Karanga in the Mberengwa region indicates that the ritual is also performed for women who have had children because women play a significant role in the communication process among the ancestors. The *kurova guva* ceremony usually occurs about one year after the person has died.

The rituals described by Zhuwawo take place among the people who live near the Roman Catholic mission at Chishawasha which was established in 1892. Zhuwawo (pp. 5–8) outlines how the missionaries established control over the people of the region by developing model Christian villages and establishing schools. The missionaries enforced attendance at mass and punished people for participating in traditional rituals. This attitude has changed over the past thirty years and now the Roman Catholic Church has attempted to incorporate aspects of the traditional ceremonies into their own liturgy. The priest even participates at some points in the traditional *kurova guva* ritual.

What Zhuwawo describes, therefore, should not be regarded as a 'pure' example of Shona Traditional Religion since the original practices have been influenced by Christianity for 100 years. Nor should the rituals be understood as anti-Christian since ways have been developed to assimilate Christian words and symbols into them.

These basic background facts are needed to place our use of the ceremonies portrayed by Zhuwawo into an appropriate context. We want to avoid, however, too many comments on the meaning, purpose, function and role of the ancestors prior to our descriptions of the ritual since such comments may distort the phenomena. Consequently, we apply the phenomenological steps to the case study in the following ways:

Step 1: Performing epochē. Following Zhuwawo's accounts, we will attempt to bracket out any pre-conceived personal notions about the value, truth, purpose, or meaning of the ritual. In addition, references to previous academic theories on this subject will be limited.

Step 2: Performing empathetic interpolation. We will try to see the ritual from a believer's point of view. Where this is confusing, we may be required to interpolate the descriptions into our own experience in order to foster empathy.

Step 3: Maintaining epochē. We will be careful to avoid judgements on any truth claims contained in the ritual. Whereas the adherent may believe literally what is being described, we will bracket those beliefs and make no comment on the actual state of affairs.

Step 4: Describing the phenomena. We are aided in our descriptions by the fact that as an observer Zhuwawo was Shona-speaking and an African. He had, therefore, an advantage over the Westerners who have described similar rituals since often they do not know the language nor share an intimate connection with the culture. We should be cautious in using Zhuwawo's field material, however, since he was also a Roman Catholic priest. We need to filter out from his work, therefore, any words or phrases which may tend to interpret the ritual rather than describe it.

Step 5: Naming the phenomena. At this stage, we will endeavour to draw out meanings from the descriptions so that an understanding of this particular ceremony will help our understanding of rituals and other phenomena in general.

The preparations

The first step in the ritual involves a series of preparations. The family elders must consult a sacred practitioner called a *n'anga* who is able to tell them if any obstacles stand in the way of proceeding with the arrangements. The *n'anga* is able to communicate with the ancestors to determine if they know of any reason the deceased person may not be brought home and join them as an ancestor (*mudzimu*).

Zhuwawo does not provide a description of an actual consultation with a *n'anga*. Rather, he cites a person he interviewed who said that the *kurova guva* ritual can be performed only if a *n'anga* has been consulted so that the descendants will be made aware 'if there is anything that needs to be put right before the actual ceremony can be performed' (p. 11). The *n'anga* is able to determine what caused the death of the person and to warn the people if the performance of the ritual will incur any danger. The *kurova guva* ritual is dangerous, says Zhuwawo's informant, if 'the spirit of the deceased is an evil spirit' or if he 'did not die a normal death' (p. 11).

Once the decision has been made to conduct the ritual, further preparations are required. Zhuwawo says that two or three people take charge of these preparations which begin with the placing of millet on a wooden plate followed by a comment addressed to the spirit of the deceased: 'Now look, (name of the deceased), we have brought this millet so that we may purify you and enable you to join the spirits of your paternal and maternal ancestors, and that you may come to guard your living family' (p. 11). The millet is soaked in water until it germinates, then dried out in the sun, then ground into a form suitable for the brewing of the beer to be used in the ritual. The actual brewing of the beer begins on the Monday of the week the ceremony is to take place. During the week, young people come together to sing joyful songs and to dance. On Friday evening, the first pot of beer is consumed while the family members play traditional musical instruments, such as *mbira* and rattles, and sing songs. One song recorded in the ceremony described by Zhuwawo is a traditional hunting chorus with the words repeated, 'My dog has gone, all alone without anyone following it' (p. 12). The people sing songs and drink the first pot of beer until around midnight when they go to bed to be ready for the beginning of the *kurova guva* ritual the following day.

The ritual

On Saturday an animal is chosen (usually a bull) which is dedicated to the spirit of the deceased and to the other ancestral spirits. The dedication, which is normally done by a brother or cousin of the deceased, contains the following words: 'Look, (name of the deceased) and you all his forbearers [*sic*], this is the relish which we have prepared for the people who have gathered here' (p. 13). The animal is then killed, skinned, cut into pieces, cooked and served along with maize meal (*sadza*) for everyone to eat.

Just before sunset, a few close relatives and the person whom Zhuwawo calls 'the master of ceremonies' (the *sahwira*) go to the graveyard where the deceased is buried (p. 13). Although Zhuwawo does not indicate who the *sahwira* is, we should note for the sake of clarity that this person is a 'ritual' or 'funeral' friend who in most cases has been a long associate of the deceased (Hodza and Fortune, 1975, viii). Bourdillon (1987, 61) adds that, strictly speaking, the *sahwira* is a person unrelated to the deceased who may be the senior member of a family which has had a long tradition of the *sahwira* relationship with the family of the deceased.

The procession to the graveyard is led by the *sahwira* and includes a woman carrying a pot of beer on her head. When the group reaches the graveyard, the *sahwira* takes the pot of beer, pours it on the grave of the deceased and announces, 'This is the beer we have brewed for you' (p. 13). The *sahwira* then picks up a handful of soil from the grave and places it on a piece of broken pot called a *chizenga* while he says, 'We are taking you home today so you may look after your family and other relatives. Do not trouble them' (pp. 13–14).

The group then returns home carrying the *chizenga* and singing songs of bravery. The group is met by people at the homestead. The men join the procession waving spears, hunting axes and other weapons and acting out scenes of war or hunting. These dramatic representations are accompanied by the women who make a high-pitched ululation. While this is going on, the *sahwira* walks slowly towards the hut or house of the deceased person. When he reaches the door, the singing, dancing and ululating cease. The *sahwira* pauses, enters the house or hut, and places the *chizenga* containing the soil from the grave on the floor.

Saturday night is a time of celebration with different types of songs being sung until dawn. One type (called *jiti*) is usually led by the youth. The music is accompanied by the fast beating of three drums. A circle is formed and the people take turns dancing inside of the circle in time with the rhythm of the drumming, high-pitched singing and hand-clapping. They sing simple songs widely known among the participants. Church songs are also included in the celebrations. A third type of song is called *ngondo* which is traditionally sung by men and women elders. Their singing is accompanied by the music of the *mbira*, rattles and the low beat of drums. Zhuwawo says the singing stops occasionally to allow the people to rest and to drink beer or a specially prepared non-alcoholic beverage (p. 15).

In the midst of these celebrations, the *sahwira* imitates characteristics of the deceased in a dramatic and humorous way. Zhuwawo says this drama 'provides a lot of laughing' (p. 15). The *sahwira* also makes accusations against members of the family such as calling some thieves or prostitutes. Those accused respond in a joking manner which adds to the drama. The singing, dancing and joking go on all night. Zhuwawo observes, 'Nobody is expected to sleep that night' (p. 15).

At dawn on Sunday, the *sahwira* and some members of the family return to the grave of the deceased. A close male relative cuts a branch from a tree, puts it over his shoulder, and carries it to the grave. At the grave another close male relative says to the maternal and paternal ancestors: 'You have done your part in purifying (name of the deceased). Now (name of the deceased) has become an ancestor and guards his descendants.'

The *sahwira* then motions to the male relative carrying the branch to approach the grave. Zhuwawo records, 'He thrashes the branch on to the grave and runs away out of the graveyard, pulling the branch behind him' (p. 15). The people then trot behind him singing traditional songs with some men whistling and the women ululating.

This is followed by a large meal on Sunday consisting of *sadza* and meat (beef, goat and chicken) which is prepared by the daughters and sisters-in-law of the deceased. Plentiful beer is also available.

Concluding ceremonies

The Sunday meal is followed by an event called *nhaka* (the inheritance ceremony) which determines what happens to the widow (or widows) and the belongings of the deceased. Bourdillon (1987, 215) explains: 'Each of the deceased's widows is expected to accept the inheritor or some other close kinsman of her late husband, possibly a senior son by another wife, as her husband, who in turn accepts responsibility for the widow and her children.' The widow, however, may object to any of those offered and, again according to Bourdillon, is requested to choose her new husband. 'If she objects to all her late husband's agnates, the marriage is readily dissolved.'

Zhuwawo does not go into detail concerning the events which follow. Bourdillon tells us that once the inheritor has been chosen and the senior widow has agreed to accept him as her husband, a ritual follows in which the inheritor and the senior widow sit on a mat together and receive token gifts from each person present as a sign that they have accepted him in his new role. Bourdillon notes that the inheritor then 'becomes responsible for the estate of the deceased which, in consultation with the deceased's sister, he is expected to distribute equitably to appropriate kin' (p. 215).

The whole of the *kurova guva* ceremony is concluded with a ritual called *kudzuruwa* which actually seals or closes the grave of the deceased. This usually occurs on the Saturday or Sunday after the *kurova guva* ceremony. On the chosen day, the *sahwira* goes to the grave with two pots of beer which are carried on the heads of two women. He also brings some undigested food found in the stomach of a slaughtered goat (*chinzvinzvi*). At the burial site, the *sahwira* removes any objects from the grave and moulds the earth into a well-compacted shape. The women approach the grave with the pots of beer into which the *sahwira* mixes the undigested food from the goat. He then pours the mixture over the grave, smearing it smoothly until the entire grave is sealed (p. 16). This act concludes the *kurova guva* ceremonies.

Phenomenological analysis of the ceremony

In this case study, efforts were made to apply Steps 1 to 3 of the phenomenological method. The endeavour to suspend prior judgements (*epochē*) is evidenced by the descriptive manner in which the ceremony is presented. Moreover, the descriptions are told 'from the inside' and this enables the reader to imagine what it would feel like to be a participant in the events as they unfold. This empathetic state is interpolated through references to singing, dancing, joking and celebrating which are contrasted with quiet and sombre moments. These activities can be translated into the experience of people from most cultures. In addition, no truth verdicts were made on the reality contained in the descriptions as efforts were made to maintain *epochē*.

We see in Zhuwawo's descriptions, however, that there are inherent limitations in applying these stages of which the student should be aware. For example, as we sought to follow Zhuwawo through the details of the various rituals, it became evident that we needed to refer frequently to previous literature on the subject. This tells us that we cannot ignore prior research and that the student should not think that *epochē* justifies a rejection of other scholarly contributions to the field from within various disciplines. The primary reason for trying to limit the impact of previous work is to enable the observer to take a fresh look at the phenomena free from the presuppositions under which the research may have been previously conducted. But one must be familiar with the literature on the subject if only to question prior methodologies and academic predispositions.

Moreover, the descriptions offered by Zhuwawo are themselves selected under certain preconceptions. His overall intention in his thesis was to compare the *kurova guva* ritual among the Vashawasha people with the Roman Catholic teaching on life after death. As a result, his descriptions were chosen in order to facilitate that comparison. This may explain why he emphasized what went on at the grave but tended to ignore the details of the inheritance ritual. There is nothing wrong with this, but the student should note that every scholar begins with some idea of what he wants to discover or at least what he suspects he might discover.

In Step 4, the actual descriptions of the phenomena are presented. The endeavour to avoid obvious interpretations while describing the rituals generally seems to be successful. Nevertheless, we find in Zhuwawo's interview with a person describing the consultation with the *n'anga* the words 'evil' and 'normal'. Such terms carry certain connotations in English which may not have been meant in the original. It would have been better, therefore, to have used descriptive language. Instead of saying 'evil spirit', Zhuwawo might have said a spirit which intends to do harm to members of his or other families. A 'normal' death might have been called 'dying of a disease in old age' as opposed, for example, to being the victim of attacks directed by spirits who are unknown to the deceased's family or who represent a family which believes that the deceased or his family were responsible for what they perceive as an injustice.

In Zhuwawo's descriptions of what occurs at various stages in the ritual, frequently too much is assumed of the reader's prior knowledge — particularly with respect to visual symbols. We do not know if any art adorns the beer pots, what colours are used in various symbols or in the clothing of the participants, or if the processions to and from the grave are orderly or not. In addition, we know very little about the *sahwira* as a sacred practitioner in the rituals: why he is chosen, how is he selected? Although descriptions must not be interpretations, they need to be loaded with detail so that the reader can imaginatively see and feel the phenomena.

Although our summary of the *kurova guva* ritual among the Vashawasha people is based entirely on Zhuwawo's work, with the exception of the points noted above, some comments in the original thesis which seem to interpret rather than describe the data have been edited out. This was done to demonstrate how one could endeavour, as far as possible, to follow the phenomenological method. Material which was removed from the original text but which demonstrates what ought not to be included in Step 4 is listed below.

1. 'There should be a joyful atmosphere in the family so that the spirit of the deceased may find it favourable to join the family.'
2. 'The Friday evening which is dedicated to *ngondo* music is believed to appease the ancestors so that they may be ready to welcome the spirit of the deceased.'
3. 'The relationship between the living and the departed is fulfilled in the sharing of the beast.'

Example 1 above clearly interprets the data. The joyful atmosphere may indeed be required to encourage the spirit to come home, but it is not explicitly stated in the phenomena and other interpretations are possible. This statement should occur at a later stage.

Example 2 uses a value-laden term. To appease carries the connotation that the ancestors are unfriendly, angry, capricious, easily offended and negative. If this is true, the phenomena must provide the support for such a conclusion. In this case, they do not or we have inconclusive data on which to make such a judgement.

Example 3 is a comment to explain the killing of the beast and the distribution of the meat. It sounds strangely Christian, particularly in speaking of a 'fulfilled' relationship and a 'sharing of the beast'. Language must be chosen carefully so as to avoid obviously distorting interpretations, even though we know that the observer can never provide 'pure' descriptions of what has occurred.

Step 5. Naming the phenomena

Out of the variety of events described by Zhuwawo, the phenomenologist seeks common names which can be used to classify, discuss, understand and find meanings within the material presented. This stage is similar to the act of perception in everyday life in which an observer mentally organizes the chaotic data of experience in an orderly and comprehensible way. The act of ordinary perceiving requires that prior linguistic concepts be employed by the observer when he describes what he sees. As noted in Chapter Two, this demonstrates an inevitable limitation to employing *epoché* since the observer already has a certain frame of understanding in place when he uses language to describe and name the phenomena.

I have indicated earlier, also in Chapter Two, that, following Hall, Pilgrim and Cavanagh, we will be classifying the phenomena of religion as myths, rituals, sacred practitioners, art, scripture, morality and beliefs. Although these categories are discussed in detail in Part II of this book, we will identify them in the context of Zhuwawo's descriptions in order to demonstrate how names are assigned to phenomena at this stage in the method.

The preparations. The observer perceives the following things at the preparation stage for the *kurova guva* ceremony:

1. The people consult a *n'anga.*
2. The *n'anga* consults the spirits.
3. The *n'anga* relays the information to the people.
4. The people act on information from the *n'anga.*
5. Millet is placed on a wooden plate.
6. Words are addressed to the deceased.
7. The millet is brewed.

Activities 1, 2 and 3 introduce the category of the *sacred practitioner,* one who plays an important role in society because of his special connection to the sacred and who relays information otherwise unknown to the people. Activity 4 might be called *morality,* what the people should do in order to fulfil the requirements communicated by the practitioner. Activities 5, 6 and 7 form a *ritual,* including sacred materials used and sacred words uttered in a particular way at a particular time. The words convey a *belief* about the relationship between the people and the spiritual world.

The terms sacred practitioner, morality, ritual and belief, although containing meanings already assumed by the observer and thus needing further analysis, are generally descriptive terms through which the activities may be discussed and understood. By naming the phenomena in this way we are able to discover what, for example, represents the sacred in this context, how the practitioner communicates with it, and how he communicates its meaning to the people.

The ceremony. The observer could list the following phenomena within the *kurova guva* ritual in various stages as they occur:

Stage 1.

1. An animal is chosen.
2. The ancestors are told about the animal.
3. The animal is killed by the in-laws of the deceased.
4. The meat is shared in a meal under the direction of the *sahwira.*

Stage 2.
5. A small group goes to the grave led by the *sahwira.*
6. A pot of beer is carried to the grave on the head of a woman.
7. The beer is poured on the grave.
8. The deceased is told the beer is for him.
9. Soil from the grave is placed on a broken pot.
10. The deceased is told he is being brought home.
11. The group processes home singing.
12. They are greeted by men who use dramatic gestures acting as warriors or hunters and by women ululating.
13. The *sahwira* places the broken pot inside the house of the deceased.

Stage 3.
14. Dancing, singing and drinking continue all night.
15. Jokes are played on family members by the *sahwira.*

Stage 4.
16. A small group goes to the grave in the morning led by the *sahwira.*
17. A close male relative who carries a branch from a tree over his shoulder is also included in the group.
18. The branch is beaten on the grave.
19. The male relative runs away from the grave dragging the branch to the homestead.
20. The others trot behind him.

Stage 1 of the ceremony introduces the *ritual* killing of an animal and sharing it with the participants. Some scholars would call this sacrifice, but the connotations of the term suggest data inconsistent with the descriptions. The ritual involves *sacred practitioners*: the one who dedicates the animal (a brother or cousin of the deceased), the ones who kill the animal (the in-laws), the one who gives instructions on the preparation and distribution of the meat (the *sahwira*). These practitioners adopt different roles in the ritual of the dedication, killing and distribution of the animal, all of which are priestly in nature.

Stage 2 includes a *ritual* with sacred objects (the pot of beer, the soil and the broken pot) and a central *sacred practitioner* (the *sahwira*). *Art* plays a fundamental role in these activities through the broken pot, through singing and dancing, and through drama. A specific *belief* is uttered when the spirit of the deceased is told he is being brought home to guard the family.

The *sahwira* then acts out characteristics of the deceased's life and personality (Stage 3). The songs sung at the celebration, such as the hunting choruses, may also reflect aspects of his life. Drama and song, therefore, build up an oral tradition about this particular ancestor who may be remembered by name for up to four generations. The rituals themselves, moreover, continue to be performed according to oral traditions in similar ways from generation to generation. Oral traditions correspond largely to the function of *scriptures* in other societies where myths, rituals, beliefs and moral codes are recorded in written form.

The ability of the *sahwira* to suspend the normal rules of social etiquette and to accuse family members of committing anti-social deeds contains elements of a cosmogonic *myth*. The singing, dancing and joking might represent an end of one time (the life of the deceased) and the beginning of a new time (the deceased becomes an ancestor) just as at the very beginning of the world something new and orderly emerged out of chaos. Although no myth is specifically recorded in this context, the role of the *sahwira* is clearly one of creating chaos corresponding to the general atmosphere of revelry.

This night is followed by a return to the grave at dawn (Stage 4) and by symbolically bringing the spirit home through beating the grave with a branch from a tree. As Zhuwawo notes, this branch comes from the forest and may symbolize the chaos, darkness and danger which exist outside the village homestead. The forest thus stands for a primeval disorder which reasserts itself at death and which is dispelled by the act of bringing the spirit home who now re-assumes an orderly life as guardian of his family. The ritual activities of Stages 3 and 4 are typical of cosmogonic myths and thus suggest the existence of these myths although they may not be explicitly stated or even consciously known by the adherents.

Concluding ceremonies. The specific data observed in the concluding phases of Zhuwawo's descriptions are:

Stage 1.
1. The wife decides whether or not to marry one of her husband's brothers.
2. Possessions of the deceased are distributed among the family members.

Stage 2.
3. The *sahwira* leads a group to the grave, including two women each carrying a pot of beer on her head.
4. Undigested food from a slaughtered goat is mixed with the beer.
5. Burial objects are removed from the grave.
6. The beer mixture is poured on to the grave.
7. The grave is moulded and sealed with the beer mixture.

Stage 1 of the concluding phase consists of a *ritual* which enforces the rules of the society and thus imposes *moral* sanctions on the community. Implicit in this moral 'ought' are the responsibilities of family members for one another, particularly for the widow or widows and her children. Stage 2 consists of a *ritual* full of symbols: the beer, the internal organ of a goat, the smearing of the substance on the grave. Each part of the ritual suggests *soteriological beliefs* (beliefs about salvation) relating to the well-being of the community by focusing on the threat to the body in the grave from outside forces and the transition from life to death to life.

Significance of naming the phenomena

From the phenomena described in the initial, central and concluding phases of the *kurova guva* ceremony, we have identified the following classifications: myths, rituals, art, oral traditions (scripture), sacred practitioners, beliefs and morality. These categories become significant as they help the observer see into the meanings of each type of activity. In this case, for example, we could look closely at the role of the *n'anga* in the preparation phase and attempt to understand what he communicates to the family and how he obtains his information. From this, we would build a picture of the *n'anga* as what we will describe later as a shamanistic/priestly type of sacred practitioner. We could then compare his role in the ritual with the *sahwira* who functions at times as a prophetic type. In this way, we would begin to see into the meaning or essence of the sacred practitioners within this specific ritual. This would be repeated for each classification derived from the phenomena. This stage demonstrates clearly that the observer actively engages with the phenomena he is describing. We have seen this already when noting the observer's choice of data to describe. We also see this in how the parts of the ritual have been organized. No stages as such exist inherently in the phenomena; they are placed there by the observer to help organize the material and to present it in a coherent way.

But beyond these somewhat obvious ways in which the observer intrudes into the phenomena and their presentation, seeing into their meaning requires him to interact even more significantly with the phenomena. For example, to call the various participants in the ritual activities sacred practitioners requires a clear presupposition that one can assume the sacred role by virtue of a specific function performed within a ritual and thus that the ritual itself (in this instance) determines the practitioner's sacredness. Or to describe the forest as a symbol for chaos and hence recalling a cosmogonic myth requires a creative interpretation of the material by the observer which cannot be said to exist intrinsically within it.

The phenomenological method, therefore, as we have noted earlier, fundamentally uses the methods of *epochē*, empathetic interpolation, and the maintaining of *epochē* in order to produce descriptions which will allow the scholar to interact creatively with the phenomena in order to derive fresh insights or new meanings of religious data. Figure 4.1 illustrates how this process has been applied to this case study.

Figure 4.1: THE FIRST STAGES OF THE PHENOMENOLOGICAL METHOD APPLIED
TO THE *KUROVA GUVA* CEREMONY

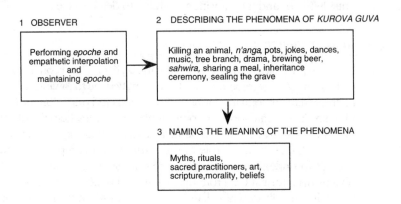

By becoming aware of his own presuppositions, the scholar endeavours to suspend his prior judgements, or at least to limit their impact on his observations. By doing this, he seeks, as far as possible, to cultivate a feeling for what, in this case, the Vashawasha people will be experiencing in the *kurova guva* ceremony. Conscious of the fact that he is always prone to interpret the data, he describes the phenomena carefully, striving to avoid either denotative or connotative distortions. By actively engaging with the phenomena, he sees into their meaning which enables him to form classifications which in turn form the basis for his understanding.

Using the case study in further phenomenological stages

To take the case study of the Vashawasha people beyond Step 5 would lead to a description of the interrelationships between the various classifications and their processes. We will already be aware of some of these relationships. For example, myths are implied in rituals which in turn involve artistic gestures, drama, dance, singing and visual representations. Rituals also use mythic symbols in gestures and dramatic activity such as the beating of the grave with the branch and dragging the branch back to the homestead. The sacred practitioner is central to the performance of rituals and to the communication of moral expectations. The oral traditions of the family are preserved in the rituals from generation to generation. Beliefs are either explicitly stated or implicitly contained in the rituals, songs, dances and mythic symbols. Once we see into the meaning of specific categories, therefore, we are able to specify how they are related.

We also note a process of movement from life to death to life operating within the ceremony. This process is part of the health and well-being of the community as a whole and thus involves other processes such as family interactions, the explanation of misfortune and death and the preservation of a stable social and cosmic order.

Historical processes can also be observed. Although we did not draw attention to the impact of Christianity on the traditional ceremony, it is evident at many places. The bull which is killed is blessed by a priest. The sharing of the meat and *sadza* carries a connotation for the Catholic community of the Eucharistic sharing of bread and wine. The *nhaka* ritual allows the woman to choose whether or not to marry her deceased husband's brother, a choice which will be influenced by Western values, in some cases perhaps by urbanization, and by legislation on succession and inheritance. Any description of the *kurova guva* ceremony of the Vashawasha people, therefore, must note that current practices reflect the process of the incorporating of Christian and Western influences into traditional practices.

Once the interrelationships and processes among the phenomenological classifications have been noted (at least in part), we are able to derive their larger comparative meanings based on the paradigmatic model of Step 7. Variations occur between the rituals, mythic symbols, the roles of sacred practitioners and other phenomena of the religious practices of the Vashawasha people and other Shona-speaking traditions within Zimbabwe. Similarities between these traditions should also be noted so that the meaning of the Vashawasha myths, rituals, sacred practitioners, oral traditions, art, morality and beliefs can be incorporated into a classification called Shona Religions which shares many resemblances with African traditional religions in general.

This larger African tradition can then be placed alongside other religious traditions according to the paradigmatic model so that the meanings and use of the phenomenological classifications within various traditions can be described and compared and so that the core concern of African traditional religions can be deciphered.

This procedure does not prescribe the content of any of the phenomena nor does it define the overriding principle of African religions; instead it offers a method for 'seeing into' them. Obviously, myths and rituals will differ within traditions, but the pattern of their use will remain consistent. Beliefs will describe sometimes contradictory pictures of the unrestricted value, but their function and types will be consistent according to the model. It would be possible, therefore, to compare the beliefs implied in the Vashawasha *kurova guva* ritual with, for example, the beliefs contained in a Hindu purification ritual where people bath in the sacred river Ganges. It would also be possible, on the basis of the paradigmatic model, to derive and compare the core concern of African traditional religions with Vaishnavite Hinduism. The purpose of the paradigm, -therefore, is to enable these comparisons to occur and ultimately lead to Step 8 which posits the eidetic intuition into the meaning of religion in general.

Summary

In this chapter, we have examined a specific ritual of a Zimbabwean religious tradition in order to exemplify how the phenomenological stages can be applied. We have emphasized the need to suspend judgements, to attend to detail, and to form classifications of the phenomena while at the same time noting the limitations in each of these stages. We have also described how the observer can see into the phenomena of that tradition (including its relations and processes) in order to derive from them the structures and patterns which can be used to compare and contrast them with other religious traditions. To test the process at any level requires returning to the phenomena to determine if they support the conclusions the observer has achieved.

With this case study in mind, we move to Part II of this book to explore the meanings of the phenomenological categories as they have been developed out of research conducted by many scholars on the world's living and archaic religious traditions. Although many examples derived from the phenomena are offered in Part II, we assume, in the light of the limitations noted in the preceding chapters, that efforts to apply the first five steps in the phenomenological method have been conducted prior to arriving at the meanings offered for each of the classifications.

References

BOURDILLON, M. F. C.   1987   *The Shona Peoples* (Gweru, Mambo Press, 3rd edn.).

HODZA, A. C. (comp.) and G. Fortune (ed.)   1975   *Shona Registers Volume I* (Harare, Univ. of Zimbabwe, Dept. of African Languages).

KILEFF, C. and P. Kileff (eds.)   1988   *Shona Customs* (Gweru, Mambo Press).

PARRINDER, E. G.   1981   *African Traditional Religion* (London, Sheldon Press).

SAMKANGE, S.   1968   *Origins of Rhodesia* (London, Heinemann).

ZHUWAWO, C.   1990   'An Investigation of Vashawasha *Kurova guva* Ceremony and the Catholic Teaching on the Life after Death' (Harare, Univ. of Zimbabwe, Dept. of Relgious Studies, Classics and Philosophy, BA(Hons.) dissertation).

Questions and Activities

Questions for discussion

1. In the descriptions of the *kurova guva* ritual presented in this chapter, what words might suggest interpretations of the data rather than pure descriptions?
2. Cite evidence for or against the claim that the presenter effectively performed *epochē* and maintained it throughout.
3. What more would you like to have known about the ritual in order to have achieved a deeper understanding of it?
4. Where do you find suggestions of Christian influence in the accounts of the ritual? Is it possible to attain an untainted description of a traditional African ceremony?
5. What obstacles stand in the way of comparing the *kurova guva* ceremony with a Hindu purification ritual?

Projects and activities

1. Either attend an actual African ritual or read about one in a book. Describe the phenomena observed or read about, name them, and then write a paragraph for each describing their meaning for the believers.
2. Read a short section from either the *Chandogya Upanishad* or from the *Tao Te Ching*. Summarize the main content. Identify from the writings any phenomena, name them, and then suggest what they mean. At the conclusion of your paper, indicate if you think written scriptures can function as effectively for phenomenological analysis as actual observations of religious activities.
3. Attend any religious activity as an observer. As you are witnessing what is occurring, write down briefly what you think the believers are experiencing. After the activity is concluded, share your observations with one of the participants asking if it accurately portrays what he/she experienced. Write a short paper on the results of this exercise.

PART II
The Phenomena

Chapter Five
Myths and Rituals

Among the classifications of the phenomena, certain categories in particular tend to complement one another and thus add understanding to their meaning and use across religious traditions. In the next four chapters we apply the paradigmatic model (Step 7 in the phenomenological method) to consider the meaning of several of these classifications together while remembering that all of them are interrelated and in process. Two types of phenomena which are closely connected are myths and rituals. In this chapter, we look at the interpretation of myths and rituals in the works of Mircea Eliade, Ninian Smart and Joseph Campbell and then test their conclusions against a case study based on late nineteenth-century accounts of certain myths and rituals among Alaskan Eskimos.

Eliade: The non-homogeneity of space and time

One of Mircea Eliade's most important works is entitled *The Sacred and the Profane* (1959). It carries the sub-title *The Significance of Religious Myth, Symbolism and Ritual within Life and Culture*. As this title suggests, Eliade regards myths and rituals as symbols of the sacred as understood from the point of view of the believer.

For Eliade the sacred is defined largely as the absence of the profane. It is delineated into the aspects of space and time so that one may speak of sacred and profane space and sacred and profane time. Myths and rituals operate within sacred space and time and hold a central place in the life of religious man (*homo religiosus*) (p. 15).

Both sacred space and time are non-homogeneous, that is, not of the same kind as other space and time. What differentiates them is a hierophany, a manifestation of the sacred told in myths and re-enacted in rituals. Profane space and time, by contrast, are homogeneous, unbroken by sacred manifestations and hence lacking any fixed centre or point around which people can derive meaning for life (pp. 20–6, 68–9).

Religious people tell stories in the form of myths describing how the original, formless, unstructured, chaotic and hence homogeneous space became formed, structured, ordered and non-homogeneous with fixed centres. Eliade calls this the founding of the world, told and re-told in mythic language. He thus calls the principal type of myth a *cosmogonic myth* (a myth which tells of the origin of the cosmos) (pp. 29–30).

Religious people tell the sacred cosmogonic myths over and over again.

As they do so, they create a sacred time, ritual time, when the myth comes to life, is re-enacted, and thus transforms the lives of the believers. In ritual, the people are able to go back to the origin of their world, to experience the creation of order out of chaos, and to find themselves renewed. The ritual occurs in a sacred space which is set apart by symbols making that space different from other space and hence an appropriate place for the ritual to occur (pp. 69–70).

Rituals, therefore, possess the characteristic of being repeatable according to a fixed pattern using symbols which are derived from and relate to the myth. The symbols may come in the form of words, gestures, drama, pictures, images, or many other forms or combinations of these. The myth is incorporated into the ritual repetitions, sometimes explicitly and at other times as a background assumption depending on the type of ritual being performed. Some rituals, for example, are calendrical, occurring at various times in the year and often relating to a people's need for subsistence, such as hunting, planting and harvesting. Some are life-cycle rituals occuring at birth, puberty, marriage and death. Others are crisis-orientated, conducted only when a crisis such as drought, infertility or war affects the community. All rituals, however, will re-enact the cosmogonic myth either directly or indirectly and transform the community by bringing it back into the sacred moment of its origin.

Primordial space (profane space) is characterized by the chaos of homogeneity lacking a fixed centre. With the creation of the world (told in myths), the world gains a focal point made known to the people by hierophanies which are then symbolized by sacred objects, altars, churches, trees, stones, mountains or other images standing for the sacred manifestation and the ordering of space (p. 53).

Eliade gives the example of a church. When one opens the door of a church, one enters a space fundamentally different from the space outside (pp. 24–5). For Eliade, the door represents the threshold between the profane and the sacred. In the church, one usually finds the central symbol of the cross or the crucifix which depicts the hierophany of the death of Jesus, a manifestation of the sacred which is told again and again in the sacred stories of Christians and re-enacted ritually in the Eucharistic celebration.

During the Eucharist, the believing community remembers the time of the hierophany. The priest lifts the loaf of bread or the wafer and announces, 'On the night in which he was betrayed, our Lord Jesus took bread, broke it, gave it to his disciples and said, "This is my body"'. Profane space and time are transcended in the ritual moment as believers re-experience the presence of the sacred reality.

From Eliade, therefore, we obtain the following components which comprise the relationship between myths and rituals:

1) Myths and rituals operate in sacred space and sacred time.
2) They result from hierophanies, manifestations of the sacred into profane space and time.
3) Hierophanies break the chaos of homogeneity by creating fixed points in space and time around which religious communities orientate their existence.
4) The occurrences of hierophanies are related in myths.
5) The mythic time of the hierophany is re-enacted in rituals which gain a transforming power for believers by bringing them back to the original act of creation.

Eliade's understanding of myths and rituals is shown in Figure 5.1.

Figure 5.1: ELIADE'S UNDERSTANDING OF MYTHS AND RITUALS

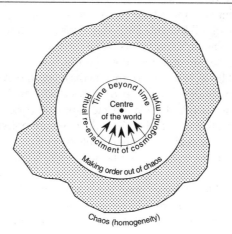

Eliade says that all religions relate myths of origins and that they re-enact them through rituals which bring renewal out of the profanity of chaotic space and time. The religious community symbolizes this by creating sacred space (the really real space) and performing rituals in a sacred time (the really real time). Eliade concludes that religious people long to live as near to the sacred as possible, that is, to live in the really real regions of sacred space and time (pp. 62–5).

Other viewpoints on myths and rituals: Ninian Smart and Joseph Campbell

Eliade bases his analysis of myths and rituals on numerous examples drawn from the history of religions, particularly from archaic religions. Two other scholars, Ninian Smart and Joseph Campbell, offer perspectives on these two forms of religious phenomena which help us see further into their meaning.

Smart (1973, 79–80) says that a myth is 'a moving picture of the sacred' which is depicted in the form of a story. As a story, it shares much in common with novels, jokes, fairy-tales, legends and historical narratives, but it is not identical with any of these. For a story to qualify as a myth, it must have two components: it must tell of sacred beings, which are usually divided into good and evil groups; and it must tell of the relationship between the sacred (the transcendent or supernatural) and the world. He thus defines myths 'as stories concerning divinities, typically in relationship to men and the world' (p. 81).

Smart adds that the function of myths is not entertainment, although they may be quite entertaining. In fact, if a story fundamentally serves as a source of entertainment for a people, it is probably not a myth but an epic tale, a piece of folklore or a fairy story. This distinction is important because it leads us to Smart's comments about rituals.

Like Eliade, Smart argues that 'the primary context' of a myth is ritual. Again like Eliade, he contends that myths relate 'the events and transactions between divinities and men' (p. 81). This is why myths generally are told in 'celebrations' such as those re-enacted annually for Christians at the festival of Christmas. It is natural that since divinities are objects of worship, stories about them will occur in a ritual context. The mythical struggle between good and evil, for example, is reflected in rituals which renounce and ward off evil.

Also like Eliade, Smart notes the relationships between myth and ritual in time and space. In rituals, he says, one time (the time of the myth) 'is represented in another time'. He cites the example of the re-enactment of the moment of Jesus' resurrection in the ritual of Easter: Christians sing, 'Jesus Christ is risen today!' (p. 87).

Moreover, by making space sacred, religious symbols actually make one place present in another. Smart recalls the example of the sacred river Ganges in India into which all other rivers are said to flow. Bathing in this sacred river ritually connects the one who has entered the waters to the river's mythic source in the distant mountain of the north.

Smart also underscores the transformative power of mythic re-enactments in rituals. He refers again to the Christian Easter story which gains its power from the fact that the mythic re-enactment is a 'replica' of the original event. A replica carries the principles of 'likeness' and 'power identity'. The re-enactment, therefore, 'is identified with the power of the enactment' (p. 92). Christian experience becomes a transforming anticipation of one's own resurrection by re-living the resurrection of Jesus. The power of the original act of creation or renewal is experienced for the believer again and again as the myth is re-told and re-experienced in rituals.

Another scholar who has written widely on the meaning of myths and rituals is Joseph Campbell. In the prologue to his four-part series on mythology, Campbell (1982, 3) identifies common themes in what he calls the mythologies present in 'the cultural history of mankind as a unit'. These themes are: 'fire–theft, deluge, land of the dead, virgin birth and resurrected hero'. Like Smart, Campbell notes that these themes are often told for entertainment in 'a spirit of play'. But when they appear in a religious context they become what Eliade calls the 'really real', or in Campbell's words, 'the verities toward which the whole culture is a living witness and from which it derives both its spiritual authority and its temporal power'.

For Campbell, myths and rituals work together by 'disengaging' the believer 'from his local, historical conditions and leading him toward some kind of ineffable experience'. Myths, therefore, possess meaning for a particular community but when they are re-enacted in rituals they transform the community by bringing it into an experience of the universal. Myths, when re-enacted in rituals, possess the unique ability 'to render an experience of the ineffable through the local and concrete', and thus 'to amplify the force and appeal of the local forms while carrying the mind beyond them' (p. 462). The specifically local character of myths and rituals thus points toward a non-specific universal (Eliade's sacred or Smart's transcendent) which stands behind them.

Are myths historical?

In everyday language, the term myth carries the connotation of the non-historical or at least of being outside historical verifiability. A common question is, therefore, 'If a story is classified as a myth, does it mean that it is not true?' The same question re-phrased asks whether or not historical events can be regarded as mythical and if they can be re-actualized in rituals.

Eliade responds to this question by drawing a distinction between religions such as Judaism or Christianity which base their sacred stories on historical events and religions such as the ancient religions of Persia or the descriptions of the activities of the gods and goddesses in Hinduism whose myths make little reference to actual events. Eliade argues that Judaism and Christianity regard time as having a beginning and an end. In the case of Judaism, Yahweh does not manifest himself in what Eliade calls 'cosmic time', a time beyond time which can be entered repeatedly through rituals. Rather, Yahweh reveals himself in historical time, a time which is irreversible and hence unrepeatable. For Christians also God manifests himself in history and thus does not reincarnate himself in rituals. Jesus lived, died and rose again *once* in history (pp. 111–12).

The biblical scholar Brevard Childs (1960, 72–3) helps us to understand Eliade's distinction between 'cosmic' and 'historical' time. He argues that myths operate in 'cosmic time' in which 'there is no actual distinction . . . between the past, the present, and the future'. He suggests that, although the original act of creation may be thought of as having occurred in some primeval past moment, 'time is always present'. Eliade contends that the primeval moment of creation is 'made' present through the recurrence of rituals which bring the believing community back into the moment when the world sprang forth fresh from the creator.

The recovery of cosmic time told in myths and re-enacted in rituals, however, is quite different from historical time. According to Childs, cosmic time 'brings nothing new in essence since the substance remains unchangeable' (p. 73). Historical time, by contrast, is defined by religious communities as the intrusion into historical moments of the sacred manifestation in a unique and unrepeatable way. This is why it can be remembered, re-told, and symbolized in rituals, but never recovered and re-entered and hence never literally re-enacted.

Eliade says that although cosmic time does not apply to religions of history, liturgical time does since this kind of time involves a remembering of historical events which can be re-enacted without being re-lived. This, he says, is quite different from actually entering into the original time of beginnings recounted in the myths of non-historical religions.

This distinction could lead us to conclude that Judaism and Christianity either do not possess myths or that part of what they teach (such as the Christian teaching on the virgin birth of Jesus of Nazareth) is actually mythical since it is non-historical. This is the position of the contemporary theologian Maurice Wiles (1977, 150) who contends that 'myths may be basically historic in origin' but 'their historical basis may be either very slight or non-existent'. For example, the myths surrounding the birth of the Buddha bear a connection to history, but the story telling of his conception by an elephant's trunk in heaven has no foundation in history. If Wiles is correct, therefore, myths can be defined as non-historical stories of divinities and of their relations with humanity and the world.

Despite his distinction between cosmic and liturgical time, Eliade does not accept this conclusion because religions which speak of historical manifestations of the divine regard history itself as sacred. The historical event defines the hierophany, the meaning of which is symbolized in ritual activities. In Judaism and Christianity, since history 'reveals itself to be a new dimension in the presence of God' (p. 111), it functions similarly in rituals as mythic time does for the non-historical religions. It is possible, therefore, to speak of historical myths, stories which affirm that certain historical occurrences actually manifested the sacred reality. The occurrences are visible as hierophanies only to the believing community and thus still retain the marks of a myth.

Ninian Smart (1973, 83), even more than Eliade, dismisses the sharp distinction made by Wiles between myth and historical occurrences. 'From a phenomenological point of view', he says, 'there is no difference in kind between an event that did happen and an event that did not happen but is believed . . . to have happened'. The phenomenologist, following *epochē*, makes no distinction between the really real and what the adherent believes to be really real. It is not phenomenologically possible, therefore, to define a myth as that which did not happen in history or as that which is scientifically implausible.

Myths are true because they are true for the believer, even if a particular community does not insist that they actually occurred within history. They are true to life and hence carry the power to transform the believer through ritual re-enactments. From a phenomenological perspective, therefore, an understanding of myths is enhanced by observing any community's use of cosmic or liturgical (historical) time and space, but whether or not the events recounted in the stories tell of real sacred manifestations is affected only by the perspectives of the religious communities themselves.

Towards the meaning of myths and rituals

From the discussion above, we are able to see into the meanings of myths and rituals as classifications of religious phenomena. We have observed that myths possess the following six characteristics:
1) A myth tells of a sacred manifestation (hierophany).
2) Myths relate stories of the origin of structures (the making of the homo-geneous non-homogeneous) through the founding of sacred space and time.
3) Myths provide for believers a picture of the sacred.
4) Myths contain stories of divine beings and their interactions with humans and the world.
5) Myths use local stories, divinities and events to point towards a universal reality.
6) Myths are true if they are true for the believer both in religions which stress the historicity of the sacred stories and those which do not.

We have observed the following six parallel characteristics of rituals:
1) Rituals manifest the sacred through a re-enactment of the original hierophany.
2) Rituals re-establish structures and thus transform and re-new the believer's existence by making space and time sacred.

3) Rituals bring the picture of the sacred to life.
4) Rituals re-enact stories of divine beings and thus re-enforce their inter-relationships with humans and the world.
5) Rituals use the local stories, divinities and events to bring the believer into the presence of the universal.
6) Rituals make the myths true by transposing the believer into the space and time of the sacred story.

Taken together, we can summarize the interaction between myths and rituals in the following three points:

1) Telling a myth itself constitutes a ritual.
2) A myth is a myth only if it is employed in a ritual.
3) The combination of myth and ritual transforms the believing community by making its space and time non-homogeneous.

Testing the meaning: An Eskimo case study

We have assumed that the phenomenological method has been employed by Eliade, Smart and Campbell to provide us with the meanings of myths, rituals and their interactions. Obviously, we cannot go back to every phenomenon to test our conclusions, but we can examine a case study. If the results listed above are correct, we should find myths and rituals working closely together. I have chosen a case study based on the accounts of the ethnologist, E. W. Nelson, who lived among the Yupik-speaking Eskimos of Alaska from 1877 to 1881 prior to the widespread incursion of Protestant missionaries into the region a few years later.

Nelson (1935b, 455–9) described in detail many of the myths and rituals of the Eskimo people who lived along the coast of the Bering Sea south of the Arctic Circle. He noted that many myths tell how the raven, a large crow common in Alaska, created all things. The following summary of one of the raven myths was related to Nelson by an old man who said he had learned it himself as a boy from a very old man.

The Myth of the Raven

The first man emerged like a seed out of the pod of a plant found on Arctic Ocean beaches similar to a pea (beach pea). He did this by straightening out his legs and bursting the pod. The man fell to the ground where he stood up a full grown man. He soon experienced an unpleasant feeling in his stomach and stooped down to drink some water from a small pool at his feet. When he looked up, he saw a dark, winged object approaching him. This was Raven who subsequently landed by the man. Raven lifted his wings, pushed up his beak like a mask, and became a human.

When he saw the first man, Raven was astonished at the sight and asked where he had come from. The man pointed to the beach pod. Raven exclaimed, 'Ah! I made that vine but did not know anything like you would ever come from it.' Raven then took the man to a hill where he formed other creatures: first mountain sheep and then a woman for the man. He then created fish, birds and other animals and taught the man how to survive in his environment. Man and woman bore a son and a daughter who married and formed the first human family.

When Raven had finished his creative acts, he returned to the beach pod from which the first man had originated only to find that three other men had emerged from it. Raven led one of these inland but he took the other two to the sea. Each was taught how to develop skills for survival: including making fire and hunting or catching sea animals.

According to Nelson, when the myth was completed the narrator always performed a concluding ritual by pouring a cup of water on the floor and saying, 'Drink well, spirits of those of whom I have told'. This comment confirms that the telling of the myth constitutes a ritual. Moreover, we know that such stories often were dramatized in dances and songs used in ritual activities. One such ritual, described by Nelson (1935a, 451–2), among the villages of the Bering Seas Eskimos is called *Ihl-u-gi* (Feast of the Dead).

This feast was held annually for those who were still awaiting the more elaborate ceremony called the Great Feast of the Dead which was conducted every five to ten years (Oswalt, 1967, 227). Nelson observed the people offering food, water and clothing to those who had died within the past year. The festival took place in what Nelson called a *kashim* (called elsewhere a *khashgii*) located at the centre of the village. It was the place where the men gathered for repairing their hunting equipment, where village social gatherings occurred and where stories were told and rituals enacted. It became a sacred place during the feast of the dead and a place of orientation around which the lives of the people were organized.

Before the ritual began, an oil-lamp was lit and placed in the *kashim* in front of the location where the deceased person normally sat on social occasions. When the ritual commenced, an old man would beat a drum slowly and rhythmically while seated in front of the main lamp in the middle of the room. All those participating would join in a long song comprising the following words:

Dead ones come here: Sealskins for a tent you will get.
Come here, do: Reindeer skins for a bed you will get.
Come here, do.

When the song was completed, the people placed a small pot of food on the floor in front of each oil-lamp and poured a little water on the same place. Then the remainder of the food was distributed and the people joined a celebration of singing and dancing.

Although the Myth of the Raven and the Feast of the Dead are not obviously interrelated, we can find evidence that the theories offered by Eliade, Smart and Campbell apply to them. The myth tells how man at his emergence from the beach pod needed water. The ritual nourishes the spirit with food and water. The myth relates how Raven created animals and instructed man how to care for them and thus how to survive. The spirit of the deceased is called in the ritual to come near and to enjoy the benefits of creation, in this case, a sealskin tent for protection and a reindeer bed for warmth.

The fact that those addressed are recently deceased and that they have yet to be honoured in the Great Festival indicates their vulnerability and their continued need for sustenance by the gifts of creation. The comment of the narrator and his pouring of ritual water after the telling of the myth further suggest that all spirits experience the same need for nourishment which the first man felt.

One of the myth's hierophanies, therefore, is water. The pool appeared at the feet of the first man. In the ritual re-enactment of this, water is provided for the spirits of the dead. Moreover, this occurs within a ritual which takes place at the centre of village life, hence it represents a structure of the universe. The *kashim* makes space non-homogeneous by fixing the centre of the world for the people and makes time non-homogeneous through rituals which overcome the barriers between the living and the dead.

The picture of the sacred reality is portrayed in terms of survival. In the myth Raven brings man to a hill where he (Raven) creates animals, teaches man how to hunt and fish and then gives him a woman. The water, food and clothing offered in the ritual correspond to this Eskimo preoccupation with survival. The fact that the people lived in a harsh natural environment and that the myths and rituals seem to focus on survival, moreover, make the stories real in the lives of the adherents since quite literally they are true to life. Finally, the fact that we can so closely connect in the ritual the spirits of the recently deceased to the cosmogonic myth of the creation of the first man provides evidence that the myth and its ritual re-enactment indicated an ineffable mystery to the Bering Sea Eskimos.

Table 5.1 provides a summary of the meaning of myths and rituals in the context of the Eskimo cosmogonic myth and the annual Feast of the Dead.

Conclusion

The descriptions and interpretations of myths and rituals and their interrelationships as presented in this chapter are not intended to be exhaustive. They stress the 'religious' aspect — Turner's 'what' which is

Table 5.1

THE MEANING OF MYTHS AND RITUALS IN THE CONTEXT OF THE ESKIMO COSMOGONIC MYTH

Meanings of myths and rituals	Raven myth and the feast
1. Each contain hierophanies.	The original water and the ritual water.
2. Non-homogeneous space and time.	The hill of the raven and his creation; the *kashim* and the ritual nourishment.
3. The founding of sacred space and time.	The order of nature and the means for survival; the symbols of survival in ritual.
4. A living picture of the sacred.	The experience of unity between the living and the dead.
5. Re-enactment of the relationship between divinities and the human.	The ritual re-enactment of the tentative nature of existence.
6. The local pointing towards the universal; the universal in the local.	The Raven, the spiritual world, nature and the delicate balance needed for survival.
7. True to life.	True to the struggle posed by a harsh environment.

interwoven into the 'milieu'. Other disciplines (see, for example, Bourdillon, 1990) would emphasize different facets within the milieu, pointing out that rituals do much more than re-enact myths and that myths cannot be explained exclusively in terms of the origins of the world and a people. For example, rites of passage perform instrumental social functions for a community, as we saw quite clearly in the *nhaka* ceremony described in Chapter Four.

We have assumed, nevertheless, that the research conducted by Mircea Eliade, Ninian Smart and Joseph Campbell has been based on a wide and accurate sampling of specific traditions according to steps five and six of the phenomenological method. This procedure has helped us arrive at conclusions regarding the religious significance of myths and rituals according to the paradigmatic model. We have tested this through a brief analysis of the Eskimo Myth of the Raven and its related ritual called the Feast of the Dead. This case study, although inconclusive in itself, suggests that our interpretations of myths and rituals are reliable and are capable of helping us build a credible interpretation of the meaning of religion itself.

References

BOURDILLON, M. F. C.   1990   *Religion and Society: A Text for Africa* (Gweru, Mambo Press).

CAMPBELL, J.   1982   *The Masks of God: Primitive Mythology* (Harmondsworth, Penguin).

CHILDS, B. S.   1960   *Myth and Reality in the Old Testament* (Naperville IL, Allenson).

ELIADE, M.   1959   *The Sacred and the Profane*, trans. W. R. Trask (New York, Harcourt, Brace).

NELSON, E. W.   1935a   'Dr. Nelson's description of Eskimo customs', in H. D. Anderson and W. C. Eells, *Alaskan Natives* (Stanford, Stanford Univ. Press), 450–5.

NELSON, E. W.   1935b   'Nelson's description of Eskimo folk tales', in H. D. Anderson and W. C. Eells, *Alaskan Natives* (Stanford, Stanford Univ. Press), 455–64.

OSWALT, W. H.   1967   *Alaskan Eskimos* (San Francisco, Chandler).

SMART, N.   1973   *The Phenomenon of Religion* (New York, Seabury).

WILES, M.   1977   'Myth in theology', in J. Hick (ed.), *The Myth of God Incarnate* (London, SCM Press), 148–66.

Questions and Activities

Questions for discussion

1) What is meant by the non-homogeneity of space and time? Give examples of how myths and rituals make space and time non-homogeneous.

2) According to Eliade, what distinguishes the sacred from the profane?

3) How could rituals transform the life of believers? Be specific.

4) Are myths true? Why or why not?

5) Why must myths and rituals be local in character? If they are local, how can they point towards the universal?

Projects and activities

1) Write down a myth from your own tradition which you have heard recited. What rituals relate to this myth? Subject the myth and one of its related rituals to an analysis similar to that in this chapter of the Eskimo Myth of the Raven and the Feast of the Dead.

2) It could be argued that the distinction between the sacred and the profane is one which applies only within Western (secular) society and does not appear in traditional societies such as are found in Africa. Write a five-page essay discussing Eliade's distinction as it applies or does not apply within a particular traditional society of your choice.

3) Attend any ritual. Take notes on any part which seems to re-enact a cosmogonic myth. Summarize your findings in a short essay.

Chapter Six
Sacred Practitioners and Art

A sacred practitioner is one who holds for the religious community a role which in various ways, times and locations connects the community with what it regards as being of unrestricted value. Frequently the function of the sacred practitioner is seen in the performance of rituals but certain of his activities may occur outside rituals. Moreover, the practitioner may simply adopt the sacred role within particular rituals or parts of rituals or perhaps may act as a practitioner only once in his lifetime. Conversely, the practitioner may take on the role of mediating repeatedly between the people and their unrestricted value. In some cases the practitioner may be regarded by the believers as being sacred in and of himself.

As a form of expressing and experiencing the sacred, art is often closely related to the sacred practitioner, who may lead the dancing, participate in the drama, wear special clothing or garments which depict the unrestricted value, or, in some cases, be the object of the art itself. Therefore, investigating how the sacred practitioner uses and is used by art helps us understand the meaning of artistic expression as a category of religious phenomena.

In this chapter we examine the phenomena of sacred practitioners and art, separately at first and then by looking at their interrelationship. We note again that these two categories, like myths and rituals, appear within other phenomena and are associated across the whole of a people's religious experience. But, like myths and rituals, the sacred practitioner is linked with art in a way which draws a close connection between the two.

The sacred practitioner: Types

For purposes of clarification, we can distinguish three types of sacred practitioners: the shamanistic/priestly type, the prophetic type and the holy person. These divisions indicate the various roles and functions of sacred practitioners and thus help us achieve an understanding of this phenomenological classification.

Shamanistic/priestly type

Mircea Eliade (1964) has done extensive research on the shaman as a sacred practitioner. He notes that actual shamans are found in Arctic regions of Asia, North America, Greenland, Iceland and Europe and in some sub-Arctic regions of Asia and North America. However, this type of sacred practitioner is not restricted to these locations since shamanistic activities represent priestly functions which are found among most religious communities (p. 6).

Eliade (1964, 4–6) defines the shaman as one who employs 'techniques of ecstasy' in order to enter into the spiritual world so that he can function as a healer, diviner, clairvoyant, director of rituals and escort of the deceased into the world of the dead. These are what we define as priestly functions. Although not all priests enter into states of ecstasy, they all employ techniques, whether learned or acquired, to release the power of the sacred for the benefit of the believing community.

I am emphasizing the shaman in this context because in shamanistic activities I discover a clear prototype for all priests. Eliade (1977, 424) explains that the shaman is 'enabled to "see" the spirits, and he himself behaves like a spirit'. In a similar way, Frederick Streng (1985, 57) defines a priest as one 'who loses his individual identity and speaks in the name of God'. In Christianity, Streng (p. 111) adds, this has meant that the priest performs 'regular devotional and sacramental services for the community' and offers 'some form of pastoral care for individuals'.

To achieve a clear picture of classical shamanistic activities, I will refer to two accounts of this phenomenon among Alaskan Eskimos, the first recorded in Wendell Oswalt's study of Alaskan Eskimos and the second as told by an Eskimo himself. The shaman described by Oswalt (1967, 222–3) was tied and bound and then placed in front of a small lamp in the *kashim*. Some people began to beat drums while others sang, inducing the shaman to enter a trance-like state. After the oil-lamp was extinguished, the shaman was able to leave his bound body, pick up the bow and arrows which had been placed beside him, and shoot the arrows into the air. The arrows travelled through the walls of the *kashim* to distant places, turned around and returned. After all the arrows had been released and had returned, the lamp was lit. The shaman could be seen still bound, but the arrows were stuck in his body. After the shaman was untied, the arrows were removed and inspected for signs of caribou blood and hair. Those with blood and hair on them could be used by the shaman to ascertain in which direction the people should move in search of caribou herds to hunt. This account demonstrates that the shaman was a person who had learned special ways of contacting the sacred reality and that he employed these skills in a priestly way to act as a mediator of well-being for the people.

My second example is taken from a book compiled by William Oquilluk (1981, 116–17), an Eskimo from the western sub-Arctic regions of Alaska. His description shows that a shaman could travel in the ecstatic state to far-off places (such as the moon) or to the world of the dead.

When a shaman was going to fly to see how things were someplace else, he had to do things in a certain way. He would lay down on the floor after he finished his special songs and doing his drumming. He had on all his clothes. Then his helpers would tie up his legs real tight with a rawhide rope. They left a piece about three feet long hang off the end of his feet. They tied a sharp hatchet to the end of that piece of rope. One of the helpers would put a pair of sealskin pants [trousers] around shamish's neck with the legs hanging over his arms. Then the helpers would pick up the shamish when he was ready and throw him on the little fire burning there. The fire would go out. The shamish's body would still be there, but his spirit was going away, flying in the air. People could hear him as he was going away from that place . . .. Sometimes he would be gone a long time. His body laid there like it was dead. Sometimes he would make a little noise. People knew he was fighting with an evil spirit then. Maybe he would get killed while he was gone. Sometimes he would be hurt and when he came back his helpers had to carry him to his house and take care of him until he felt good again. Mostly they would come back without any trouble.

From Oquilluk's description, told from the point of view of a believer, we understand why Eliade (1964, 8) described the shaman in priestly terms as the 'great specialist in the human soul'. In the light of Oswalt and Oquilluk's accounts and in view of Eliade's academic research, therefore, the characteristics of the shamanistic/priestly type of sacred practitioner can be summarized as follows:

1. The shaman–priest possesses special knowledge or experience through which he is able to make contact with the sacred.

2. The shaman–priest makes this contact in order to provide a link between the sacred and the people.

3. The link between the sacred and the people is necessary for the community's well-being and survival (sometimes understood in spiritual rather than physical terms).

Prophetic type

Like the shaman, the prophetic type of sacred practitioner adopts a mediating role, but he does so by receiving and delivering a message from the sacred reality which the people need to hear and to which a response is demanded. For example, in his book on world scriptures, Kenneth Kramer (1986, 183) defines the prophets of Israel as 'forthtellers', those who proclaimed God's message of doom for those who failed to respond and salvation for those who turned away from their disobedience. Kramer identifies three specific functions of the Hebrew prophets: they challenged the advance of pagan civilization by their unyielding demands for right conduct and moral living; they criticized rituals which had lost their moral meaning; and they re-emphasized ethical monotheism. In these ways, they became the voice for God.

For Christians Jesus can be regarded as a prophetic type within the Jewish tradition since he challenged Roman (pagan) civilization by calling for his own people's righteousness. He also criticized rituals and ritual laws which had lost their moral character. And Jesus re-emphasized the response of the people to the one God he referred to as his Father.

Muhammad, the prophet of Islam, declared himself to be a prophet in the tradition of the Jewish prophets and of Jesus. Muhammad received the definitive message from God (Allah) which overthrew Arabic paganism, challenged a weakened form of Judaism, exposed the confusion of Christians about Jesus, demanded that rituals fundamentally contain the moral call for submission and declared a pure unyielding monotheism. In this sense, he became the 'seal' of the prophets.

The Jewish, Christian and Islamic traditions, therefore, have Kramer's three points in common. But other traditions also contain elements of receiving a message from the sacred and communicating it to the people. Whereas the Jewish, Christian and Islamic traditions emphasize the one God who confronts his people, other perspectives suggest that the prophet leads the way for each person to achieve meaning and purpose in his or her own life. In this sense, the Buddha is a prophetic type of sacred practitioner because he saw into sacred reality and communicated his vision so that others might discover the path to salvation.

Siddhartha Gautama became the 'Enlightened One', the Buddha, first by recognizing that the world is full of suffering. Although his wealthy father tried to shield him from seeing this truth, Siddhartha discovered the facts of illness, old age and death. In response, he gave up all of his worldly pleasures to search for meaning. After trying other religious approaches of his day, he achieved enlightenment while meditating. His vision led to his teaching concerning the Four Noble Truths and the Eightfold Path (Percheron, 1982, 15–31).

Although the message the Buddha discovered did not occur in a context similar to the Jewish–Christian–Islamic idea of a revelation from God, it did represent a seeing into reality itself. His message, therefore, represents a word from the realm of the sacred (the unrestricted value). Moreover, the Buddha's enlightenment was not his alone: others could also experience it if they followed his teachings. In this way, the Buddha fits the prophetic type of sacred practitioner.

In the light of the above examples, the characteristics of prophetic types among religious communities can be summarized as follows:

1) A prophet receives a message from the sacred.
2) The prophet's role is to deliver the message from the sacred to the people.
3) The message is necessary for the people to hear and appropriately

respond to if they are to be saved from what the message defines as their threatening condition.

The holy person

Some sacred practitioners are sacred because they possess within themselves what the people regard as the unrestricted value. The person is sacred not just at particular moments, when in a trance or when performing rituals: the person himself becomes a hierophany.

Jesus provides an example of this type of sacred practitioner. He not only delivers the word from God, he *is* the word. For his followers, he is not just the Son of God, but God the Son. He is the second person of the Holy Trinity, one with the Father and the Spirit. Jesus is 'of the same substance with the Father' as the fourth-century Nicene Creed declares. For the believers, therefore, Jesus is the holy person *par excellence*, 'very God of very God' (Davies, 1959, 69–72).

Many followers of the Buddha also elevated him from being one who saw into the meaning of existence to one who in himself embodied and thus defined that meaning. Siddhartha Gautama made no claim to be divine but, particularly in Mahayana Buddhism (the form of Buddhism found generally in northern regions of Asia, Japan and Korea), a doctrine developed surrounding the concept of 'Buddhahood'. Siddhartha was regarded as one who incarnated in himself the heavenly Buddha and thus was able to teach others.

The philosopher John Hick (1977, 169) argues that the elevation of Jesus from a prophet to God in the Christian faith is similar to what happened with Siddhartha, who was transformed from the Buddha (Enlightened One) to Enlightenment itself. Hick explains: 'The human Gautama came to be thought of as the incarnation of a transcendent pre-existent Buddha as the human Jesus came to be thought of as the incarnation of the pre-existent Logos or divine Son.' Both Jesus and Siddhartha Gautama, therefore, can be regarded as prophetic types *and* as holy persons depending on how they are seen and understood by believers.

Another example of a holy person is found in Monica Wilson's (1959, 21–5) descriptions of the divine king Kyungu among the Nyakyusa people of Malawi. Kyungu was a big man physically who had fathered many children. At the time of her writing, Wilson says he was already old and regarded as a man of wisdom. The people treated him in a way which shows that they regarded him as divine, particularly when they protected him from misfortune. Wilson writes: 'He must not fall ill, suffer a wound, even bleed, for his blood falling on the earth would bring sickness to all the people — the whole country'. She adds that Kyungu was thought to have created food and rain. His breath, hair, nails and even the mucus from his nose kept the land fertile. By virtue of his inherent sacredness, therefore, he sustained the people.

Within all religious traditions, a holy person represents the sacred world for a people. They see in him the meaning of their unrestricted value. In his own way, therefore, a holy person, like all other sacred practitioners, mediates the sacred to the people. The holy person does this, however, by providing a direct link (a hierophany) between the people and what is most important in their existence.

Sacred practitioners: A summary

What each type of sacred practitioner holds in common is the mediating role, the fact that in some sense each practitioner enables the sacred to manifest itself to the people and enables the people to respond appropriately to that manifestation. The shaman–priest, by his entering into sacred realms, represents the people before the sacred. The prophet receives and communicates a sacred message the people must hear and respond to if they are to avoid calamity and achieve some form of salvation. The holy person is the hierophany; by being in his presence the people are in direct contact with the unrestricted value.

Each type of sacred practitioner contains aspects of the other. The shamanistic/priestly type may deliver a prophetic message, 'Do this or die!' The prophet, like Isaiah of the Hebrew scriptures or Muhammad, may also experience ecstatic seizures and thus share characteristics with shamans. Because of his special relationship with the sacred, the shaman–priest may be regarded as holy, or at least set apart from the rest of the people. The same could be said for a prophet. Holy persons, like Jesus or the Buddha, may also be prophets or may represent the people within the sacred realities. The three types discussed above, therefore, are not meant to be applied rigidly, but to serve as guidelines for understanding the roles and functions of sacred practitioners. These guidelines are summarized in Table 6.1.

Art

Art in a religious context is a broad term encompassing many ways of expressing, appreciating and experiencing the sacred. It includes songs and dances, music and rhythm, painting, architecture, drama, clothing, masks, sculpture, poetry and stories — in short, the many ways in which a people's experience of the sacred are symbolically presented and represented. Raymond Firth (1973, 15–16) says that symbols stand for (represent)

Table 6.1

THE SACRED PRACTITIONER

Type	*Characteristics*
Shamanistic/priestly	Represents the people by special techniques or knowledge which provide him with unique access to the sacred world.
Prophetic	Receives a message from the sacred which he delivers to the people without which they will be kept from achieving salvation.
Holy person	A sacred manifestation in himself who provides a direct link between the people and the sacred reality.

something towards which they point. As such, 'the symbol appears capable of generating or receiving effects reserved for the object to which it refers — and such effects are often of high emotional charge'. Frederick Streng (1985, 167) adds that art 'exposes the deepest meaning of life'.

Since art in religion symbolizes or stands for the sacred, it provides us with a direct view into the believer's religious experience. Through painting or drama or song, the observer senses what it means to be an adherent within a particular tradition. In this light, W. Cantwell Smith (1978, 173) calls art an 'expression' of a people's faith which cannot be explained fully in words. The observer must enter into it and experience it.

Smith cites the following example from his own experience to underscore this point.

> On a wall of Aya Sofia in Istanbul there stands, recently uncovered, an ancient mosaic depicting the first confrontation of the courtesan Mary Magdalene and Christ. To portray Christ's face, the unnamed artist has put together a few bits of coloured stone in such a fashion as to portray, in a way that was more forceful and more effectively unified than I have met in any theological statement, what in prose I call simultaneous judgment and forgiveness.

Through art, the combination of Christ's judgement and forgiveness was communicated so the observer (Smith) could grasp its meaning in one moment better than he could ever have done by reading volumes of theological works on the subject. This exemplifies the fact that artistic expressions in religion depict and portray, often with a transforming power, what any tradition regards as the unrestricted value. Following Hall, Pilgrim and Cavanagh, we see that it does this in two basic ways: through presentational and through representational art.

Presentational art

Hall, Pilgrim and Cavanagh (1986, 78) refer to presentational art as that which immediately brings the believer into the presence of the sacred or 'invokes' that presence. Following Eliade, any artistic expression which serves as a hierophany qualifies as presentational art. For example, Eliade calls the traditional garments and masks worn by a shaman a hierophany as they bring the believer directly into contact with the sacred through the symbols depicted on what the shaman wears.

The masks of the shaman often portrayed cosmogonic myths where the raven or other animals could be both human and animal. Oswalt (1967, 230) says that such a mask 'might have an animal or a bird head on half the mask and a human head represented on the other half, the division being down the center of the mask'. Eliade (1964, 147) concludes that the shaman's costume is 'a complete symbolic system' by which the shaman 'transcends profane space and prepares to enter into contact with the spiritual world'. When the people approach the shaman wearing his artistic garments, the sacred presents itself to them.

Another example of presentational art is found in the icons of the Eastern Orthodox Christian churches. Icons generally portray holy persons and are the means whereby a believer communes directly with the sacred. Worshippers kiss the icons, direct their attention towards them in prayer and meditate on them. Any art, therefore, which *presents* the sacred so that the believer directly experiences it is presentational art.

Representational art

Art which tells a story, offers a message or conveys a truth is representational. 'As such', say Hall, Pilgrim and Cavanagh, 'representational symbols could be said to perform a more didactic or teaching function as the tradition or religion is passed on down through history' (p. 78). For example, the mosaic observed by Smith, although it struck him forcibly, represents judgement and mercy, both of which it was necessary for him to experience in order to understand the sacred as a compassionate and holy being. Believers who encounter the same mosaic, as Smith did, see in Jesus' face purity and love and thus learn about God, humanity and the Christian way of salvation. The same message might be transmitted through songs and poetry. For example, Frederick William Faber's famous hymn, a stanza of which is quoted below (Faber, 1983, 230), conveys to many Christians the same understanding that Smith obtained when viewing the Byzantine mosaic.

> There's a wideness in God's mercy
> Like the wideness of the sea;
> There's a kindness in his justice
> Which is more than liberty.

Presentational and representational art

Most art can be either presentational or representational depending on its use and understanding by the believers. For example, Michelangelo's famous paintings on the ceiling of the Sistine Chapel in the Vatican can fit into either category. His most famous painting is that of God reaching out and almost touching the finger of man at the moment of creation. One could look at that painting and immediately feel in the presence of the transcendent Creator and marvel at his majesty. That would make Michelangelo's painting *presentational*. Or one could look at it and see in it teachings about the power of God, creation out of nothing and human dependence. It would then be classified as *representational* art.

When art is used in rituals, it tends to be presentational. We have seen this with myths. Their very telling constitutes a ritual which transforms the believer by bringing him into a time beyond time, into the sacred moment of creation. One could also derive certain teachings about the sacred and understandings of the world from myths. This takes the myth out of its ritual context and makes it largely representational. This is why Hall, Pilgrim and Cavanagh contend that 'since ritual in general is more presentational, the artistic forms that play a central role in ritual are more presentational in function' (p. 79).

One further example may help to clarify how art can be both presentational and representational. The Bible of the Christian and Jewish traditions contains poems, parables, myths, teachings, sermons and many other literary art forms. When the Bible is read in a Christian worship service, it is being used as a representational art form since it is usually telling a story or offering a message. It can also be used, however, in a presentational way when, for example, it is adorned with gold at the edge of its pages, is bound with a gold or silver cover containing sacred images and when it is ritually carried towards the front of the church and placed on the pulpit. As it is brought forward, the people stand up out of respect and acknowledge the Word of God through which the sacred is made present to them.

Table 6.2 illustrates the relationship between presentational and representational art.

Table 6.2

THE RELATIONSHIP BETWEEN PRESENTATIONAL
AND REPRESENTATIONAL ART

Presentational art	*Representational art*
A hierophany.	Didactic.
Leads the believer into a direct experience with the sacred.	Helps the believer understand the sacred so that he can experience it.
Usually forms a part of rituals.	Can be separated from rituals.

NB: Most art can be presentational or representational.

The sacred practitioner and art

We have defined three types of sacred practitioner and two categories of artistic expression, noting that none of these classifications can be rigidly delineated. We now examine some of the relationships between sacred practitioners and art.

The shaman–priest and art

We have already noted that the costume worn by a shaman is a hierophany in itself — presenting the sacred directly to the believers. Drumming, singing and dancing also help induce his trance and form a part of the shaman's technique of ecstasy. A musical instrument used to assist Eskimo shamans has been described by Oswalt (1967, 220) as a 'tambourine type drum' made of seal or walrus bladder and stretched over a wooden frame varying in diameter between one and three feet. The drummer, who could either strike the rim or the centre of the instrument with a stick, produced a rhythm which was vital for the shaman to leave his body and travel to other worlds. Without art, therefore, the shaman could not perform his sacred role of mediation.

This could also be said about other priests. The Anglican or Roman Catholic priest, for example, usually wears a vestment called a chasuble when celebrating the Eucharist. This garment is often elaborately adorned with various Christian symbols and is of varying colours — gold, representing the Kingship of Christ; red, the tongues of flame of the Holy Spirit's appearance at Pentecost; purple, the blood of Christ shed on the cross; and so on. As he says the words of celebration, the priest can be seen to present Christ to the people who is symbolized through the priest's artistic vestments, but the symbols also represent beliefs of the community about Christ.

Prophets and art

The word delivered by the prophet comes in an art form, whether it is spoken or written. The Hebrew prophets, for example, used dramatic prose in order to represent the message calling for the people's repentance. In Christian churches the preacher often adopts the prophetic role by proclaiming the divine message dramatically so as to invoke a response from the people. In Islam the sacred book (*Qur'ān*) supremely presents *and* represents the word of Allah both as it was revealed to the prophet Muhammad and as it has been preserved by later generations. A brief look at the *Qur'ān*, therefore, will illustrate the relationship between prophets and artistic expressions.

Since the *Qur'ān* is literally the Word of God in a presentational art-form, it is treated with reverence. Muslims are encouraged to commit its words to memory, reciting it in its original Arabic. They have also preserved it through the use of calligraphy, an ornate type of handwriting which makes the text especially beautiful (Kamm, 1976, 7–8).

The *Qur'ān* also represents the message of Allah as delivered by the prophet in a book comprising 114 chapters called 'suras'. The word 'sura' means 'degree' or 'step' by which the believer approaches a more nearly perfect submission to God. Each chapter, therefore, contains a didactic message aimed at assisting the believer in his devotion to Allah.

Since the *Qur'ān* contains many art forms such as myths, poetry and dramatic prose, most of the suras both bring the believer directly into contact with Allah (presentational) and teach about him (representational). An example of this is found in the opening sura which Kenneth Kramer (1986, 258) calls 'the quintessence of the entire book'. Even in its English translation (Ali, 1977, 14–15), the artistic power of the words can be appreciated by the reader while at the same time helping him learn about the Islamic concept of the unrestricted value.

In the name of God, Most Gracious, Most Merciful.
Praise be to God, the Cherisher and Sustainer of the Worlds:
Most Gracious, Most Merciful:
Master of the Day of Judgement.

Thee do we worship,
And Thine aid we seek.
Show us the straight way.
The way of those on whom
Thou has bestowed Thy Grace,
Those whose (portion) is not wrath,
And who do not go astray.

These verses form a part of the Muslim's prayers five times a day. The words, initially delivered to the prophet, guide the believer into an appropriate relationship with the sacred. They show, therefore, how the prophet, as a type of sacred practitioner, uses art (both presentationally and representationally) to accomplish his role of mediating the divine word to the people.

The holy person and art

The person who himself is a hierophany often becomes the object of art — either to present the sacred directly to the believer or to represent truths about the unrestricted value which have been derived from the holy person. A good example of this is found in Buddhist art — for example, paintings, sculptures and religious objects.

In his book on Buddhism, Maurice Percheron (1982, 172-3) relates how in Cambodia images of the Buddha present a calm, serene face. The lips are clearly depicted in 'an elusive smile'. The eyes are lowered so as to appear half open and half shut. The whole image portrays one who is in deep reflection and yet filled with 'tender compassion'.

On his search for enlightenment, the believer may see in this image that which brings him into direct contact with the sacred reality. The Buddha's elusive smile and eyes half closed to the world demonstrate that he has attained inward peace. He keeps his eyes half open to the world, however, as a sign of love for those who have not yet achieved total bliss. Meditation on the sacred image, therefore, helps the seeker achieve the same experience as the Buddha discovered.

One can also understand the image as representing certain truths: each person must discover his own enlightenment; the world of suffering can be overcome only by finding the truth within oneself; peace can never be attained by attaching oneself to the world; compassion for the unenlightened keeps those who have been enlightened in this world in order to help others find the way. These concepts can be derived from a long and careful study of the Buddha's image.

As mediators between the sacred world and the human, therefore, holy

persons are depicted in art in various religious traditions in order to lead
believers directly into the presence of the sacred and/or to convey to the
believers truths about the sacred.

Summary

Our discussion of the sacred practitioner as a mediator between the sacred
and the people and of art as being presentational or representational
demonstrates how these two phenomena are closely related. The sacred
practitioner cannot mediate without art: art becomes the tool for symbolizing
the mediation.

Understanding this relationship helps us draw other connections among
the phenomena, for example, between art and myths and rituals or the
sacred practitioner's use of art in ritual. Drawing such connections forms a
part of the phenomenological structure of religion in which the student of
religion gains an understanding of the processes and interrelationships
between all religious phenomena.

References

ALI, A. Y. (trans. and commentator) 1977 *The Glorious Qur'ān* (n.p.,
    Muslim Students' Association of the United States and Canada).
DAVIES, J. G. 1959 'Christianity: The early Church', in R. G. Zaehner,
    Concise Encyclopaedia of Living Faiths (Boston, Beacon), 51–85.
ELIADE, M. 1964 *Shamanism: Archaic Techniques of Ecstasy*, trans. W.
    R. Trask (London, Routledge).
ELIADE, M. 1977 *From Primitives to Zen: A Thematic Sourcebook of the
    History of Religions* (San Francisco, Harper and Row).
FABER, F. W. 1983 'There's a wideness in God's mercy', in *Hymns and
    Psalms: A Methodist and Ecumenical Hymn Book* (London, Methodist
    Publishing House).
FIRTH, R. 1973 *Symbols: Public and Private* (Ithaca, Cornell Univ. Press).
HALL, T. W., R. B. PILGRIM and R. R. CAVANAGH 1986 *Religion: An
    Introduction* (San Francisco, Harper and Row).
HICK, J. 1977 'Jesus and the world religions', in J. Hick (ed.), *The Myth of
    God Incarnate* (London, SCM Press), 167–85.
KAMM, A. 1976 *The Story of Islam* (Cambridge, Dinosaur Publications).
OQUILLUK, W. A. 1981 *People of Kawerak* (Anchorage, Alaska Pacific
    Univ. Press).
OSWALT, W. H. 1967 *Alaskan Eskimos* (San Francisco, Chandler).
PERCHERON, M. 1982 *Buddha and Buddhism* (Woodstock, Overlook
    Press).

SMITH, W. C.   1978   *The Meaning and End of Religion* (San Francisco, Harper and Row).
STRENG, F. J.   1985   *Understanding Religious Life* (Belmont, Wadsworth).
WILSON, M.   1959   *Communal Rituals of the Nyakyusa* (London, Oxford Univ. Press).

Questions and Activities

Questions for discussion

1. What is a shamanistic type of sacred practitioner? What does it mean to say that a priest fits into this category? Discuss the Roman Catholic priest as a shaman.
2. Discuss how the Buddha and Jesus are similar and/or dissimilar as: a) prophets, and b) holy persons.
3. What does it mean to say that Muhammad is the 'seal of the prophets'?
4. Show how a *n'anga* of the Shona tradition (See Chapter Four) can be a) shamanistic/priestly, b) prophetic, c) a holy person.
5. Brainstorm a list of art objects. Identify each item on the list as presentational, representational or both.
6. What are the advantages/disadvantages of discussing the sacred practitioner and art as related classifications of religious phenomena?

Projects and activities

1. Look up the word 'ecstasy' in a dictionary. Write a short essay in which you apply the dictionary's definition to the shamanistic/priestly type of sacred practitioner as discussed in this chapter. Refer to Eliade's works in your essay.
2. If you have ever seen a person under spirit possession, write a description of what you observed.
3. Arrange for an interview with a member of an Independent or Zionist church which follows a prophet. Find out how the prophet a) received a message from God; b) how the message was delivered to the people; c) why the people believe the prophet is authentic; d) what the content of the prophet's message is.
4. Enter any church, synagogue, temple or other sacred building. Make a list of the art objects you see in the building. Try to understand each as either presentational or representational. Write a summary of your findings.

Chapter Seven

Scripture and Morality

In this chapter we examine two other classifications of phenomena and study their interrelationships. We begin with scripture, the written texts of religious traditions obtained from oral sources, and then look at morality, codes of conduct often recorded and exemplified in scripture.

The nature of scripture

The word 'scripture', as Kenneth Kramer notes (1986, 10), comes from the Latin *scriptura* and literally refers to the act of writing. It commonly denotes, therefore, the written texts of religious traditions. These texts are regarded differently among the traditions with some, such as Islam, revering the text as itself sacred and others, like Buddhism, regarding the recorded words as guides appropriate to the individual's search for enlightenment.

Although the term scripture literally refers to written texts, all texts are developed in a process incorporating oral traditions. Some religions, however, never develop written sources, but pass on their teachings, myths, rituals and moral understandings in oral form from generation to generation. From a phenomenological point of view, this does not mean that traditions with written texts are more advanced than those which do not record their basic teachings.

In his book exploring scriptures in the world's religions, Harold Coward (1988, x) argues that there is a tendency, particularly among Western scholars, to value the written word over the oral traditions. This, however, is 'characteristic of only the most recent period of Western cultural history'. Scripture, he argues, 'has been understood by more people in most times and places (other than our own period) as including both the oral and the written word' (ibid.).

The general process by which scriptures are developed follows three stages. The first stage involves the occurrence of sacred events, what, as we have seen, Eliade calls a hierophany. The second stage moves to the telling of sacred stories about the sacred event and the re-living of these events in rituals. This constitutes the oral tradition. The third stage in some traditions produces written texts which record the sacred events through the oral traditions. The process follows the steps outlined in Figure 7.1.

The order of events is depicted in this figure as it would be seen by a believer. Obviously, the development of written texts is far more complicated than this chart implies. Oral traditions change and continue to influence the

Figure 7.1: THE DEVELOPMENT OF SCRIPTURE

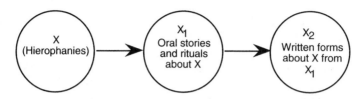

development of written texts. The written texts, moreover, frequently undergo changes often with layer on layer intertwined into a final document which may be produced over a very long period of time (as seen in the Hebraic creation story in the first chapter of Genesis) and may be influenced by ritual activities. For a believer, however, the hierophany is paramount and constitutes the source of what is spoken of and later written about.

Sacred events and oral traditions

That fact that hierophanies form the beginnings of scripture for believers as they are told and re-created in myths and rituals can see be seen clearly in Benjamin Ray's (1976, 39) description of this process among the Dinka people of southern Sudan. An important myth of the Dinka tells how in an early time, before they had become fully established as a people, a drought occurred during which their cattle starved and died. What follows in the story is a series of sacred events which eventually led the people to a more fertile land, taught them survival skills and established ritual activities connected with these methods of survival.

The sacred manifestations reported in the story include the ability of a hero named Aiwel Longar to sustain his cattle during the drought by obtaining water from beneath tufts of grass. The knowledge of how to do this was revealed to him by sacred sources (a hierophany). Longar then told the people to travel to a new land 'where there was endless grass and water and no death'. The people refused and Longar set off alone. Finally the people followed but the supreme god Nhialic set mountains and rivers in their way. The very existence of such obstacles can be defined as hierophanies since the supreme being placed them there for a purpose.

The story continues, telling how Longar stood on a high mountain to view a river which the people were trying to cross in order to enter the new land. As the people attempted to cross, Longar killed them one by one with a thrust from his fishing spear. He continued until one man named Agothyathik fooled Longar into thinking a decoy was a real person. When he realized he had been tricked, Longar attacked Agothyathik. They wrestled for a long time until both became tired. Longar then told Agothyathik to summon his people across the river. Longar gave fishing spears to some men and to others he gave war spears.

This myth stands behind the development of the priestly and warrior classes in Dinka society. Those who perform certain priestly rituals use fishing spears whereas those who engage in battle carry the war spears. The possession of the spears thus refers to the original sacred manifestations of Longar's spear-throwing, his wrestling with Agothyathik and the final establishment of the people in the new land across the river.

These sacred events are told in the oral traditions of the Dinka people and are re-enacted in their rituals. We see clearly, therefore, how hierophanies (X) are transmitted orally through their re-telling in myths and their re-enactments in rituals (X_1). The Dinka do not possess written scriptures, but their oral traditions function in a similar way as the written texts do for other religious communities.

From oral tradition to written sources

Some religious traditions record their stories, rituals and teachings in written form. They undergo a process, therefore, of developing written texts out of their oral transmissions. This process can be seen clearly in Islam which can be regarded as a classic example of a 'religion of the book'. As we have suggested, the *Qur'ān* is regarded by believers as literally the word of God, a hierophany containing the sacred message. The book itself, however, is not the sacred manifestation: the hierophany is defined as the words contained in the book.

When Muhammad received his first revelation from Allah through the Angel Gabriel, he was told to 'recite', that is, to speak out the words he had received. The words he recited were revealed by Allah. He set them to memory but, since it is believed that he was illiterate, he could not write them down. Although the Muslim tradition holds that as soon as Muhammad recited a revelation, his companions recorded it on leaves, bark, bones or whatever they could find, the *Qur'ān* itself was not completed in its final version until approximately twenty years after Muhammad's death. This explains in part why every Muslim is urged to memorize the *Qur'ān* and to recite it. The word is fundamentally oral.

The case of Islam supports Harold Coward's claim that the oral tradition has a primary place over written texts in all religious traditions. Coward argues that in most faiths the oral word is regarded as eternal. This, he says, is true of the teaching of Siddhartha Gautama who (in Mahayana Buddhism) became enlightened as an embodiment of the eternal Buddha, of the word uttered at the beginning of each Hindu cycle of creation, of the Torah which

God dictated to Moses on Mount Sinai, and of the eternal Word of God become flesh in Jesus of Nazareth (p. 165).

Why, then, did certain traditions record the sacred oral word in written texts? One answer to this is suggested by the case of Islam. Since the word itself is sacred, it came from the mouth of the prophet accurately and perfectly. This is why Muhammad's words were recorded immediately and faithfully on various objects and kept safely in a bag. No error in transmission could occur using the written method.

A second purpose for recording the word in written form is also suggested by the case of Islam. After Muhammad's death, what A. Yusuf Ali (1977, xxxiii) calls 'a furious storm of apostasy' occurred. In other words, many people began to interpret the word of God in ways which were unfaithful to its original transmission. In defence of the word, many followers were killed, most of whom knew the *Qur'ān* by heart. It was then decided, according to Ali, 'to preserve the *Qur'ān* intact in its original form against any and every kind of danger'.

In addition to the need for accuracy and to oppose heresy, some traditions, such as Christianity, needed a means of making the message coherent, organized and verifiable. The followers of Jesus thus required a record of his life, teachings and activities. Some scriptures develop, therefore, to unify the essential message into an intelligible form.

A further explanation suggested by Coward (1988, 173–4) for the development of written texts is that by writing scriptures, the sacred story becomes available to all people. When the sacred event is told in myth and re-enacted in ritual, it often comes under the control of priests or sacred practitioners. When it is written and distributed, it becomes the possession of all the people. This occurred, for example, in the Protestant Reformation which adopted the doctrine expounded by Martin Luther of the 'priesthood of all believers' and had as one of its main objectives that the Bible should become available to all people.

We conclude, therefore, that scripture is fundamentally and primarily oral and that it is told and passed on within religious communities from generation to generation. For historical, theological and practical reasons, some traditions write down the oral transmissions, a process which in some traditions (like the Hebraic) occurs over a very long period of time and includes the insertion of new interpretations of the oral tradition into the text by editors. The reasons suggested by Coward that scriptures are written rather than remaining oral are summarized below:

1. To preserve accuracy in the telling of the sacred events.
2. To guard against wrong interpretations of the sacred events.
3. To present the sacred events in an organized and unified way.
4. To make the sacred events available to all the people.

Morality

Within the scriptures of any tradition we find the moral rules, the authoritative 'oughts' of any religion. These are derived from the sacred events, told in myths and ritually re-enacted. In some traditions, the moral codes have been recorded in written form whereas in others they have remained oral. Both, however, are regarded by the religious community as providing regulations for the life of the people and as proceeding from the sacred or unrestricted value.

At this point, therefore, we can add a further dimension to the diagram demonstrating how scriptures have developed (see Figure 7.2).

Figure 7.2: THE DEVELOPMENT OF MORAL PRESCRIPTIONS

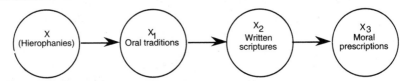

Every religion prescribes in some sense how the believer 'ought' to behave. The 'ought' is an imperative because its authority is traced back to the hierophany. To disobey the moral imperative is to disrupt life, to threaten well-being, to move away from the centre toward chaos, to counteract the ordering effect of the original sacred event.

The moral 'ought' comes in different forms in varying traditions. In the Hebrew scriptures, we see it in the form of the commandments delivered by God to Moses. The hierophany is the presentation of the law to Moses who then delivers it to his people. The law is told and recorded. It prescribes how the people are to live, lists punishments for disobedience and defines means by which forgiveness and reconciliation can be obtained.

By contrast in the Chinese tradition called Confucianism, the moral 'ought' comes not in the form of a commandment, but as advice often communicated in proverbs. Its imperative nature is nevertheless confirmed by the fact that the wise man, Confucius, is able to discern the perfect pattern for human conduct which is modelled after the ideal, what is called the will or way of heaven (*T'ien*). The Confucian hierophany is thus the wisdom of the sage who discerns the will of heaven and describes it to the people. If the people follow the teaching, harmony and peace prevail; if they ignore the wisdom of the sage, chaos and disorder will result (Graham, 1959, 370).

An example of Confucius's teaching can be seen in his advice to governmental rulers. The wisdom he offers is based on the principle of reciprocity which he described as a universal idea governing all relationships:

Govern the people by regulations, keep order among them by chastisements, and they will flee from you and lose all self-respect. Govern them by moral force ... and they will keep their self-respect and come to you of their own accord (*Analects*, II. 3; cited by Kramer, 1986, 111).

Yet another form of the moral 'ought' is seen in the caste system of India, the organization of the social order according to classifications determined by birth. The four classes of Hindu society in descending order are the *Brahmin* (priestly), the *Kshatriya* (the warriors), the *Vaisya* (vassals) and the *Sudra* (servants). The classes originated, according to Hindu mythology, from a hierophany told in one of the Hindu scriptures called the *Rig-Veda* in which the body of the god Purusha was divided up to form the various parts of society. This myth is recounted by the Indian scholar L. M. Joshi (1975, 65).

When they divided Purusha, how many portions did they make? What do they call his mouth, his arms? What do they call his thighs and feet? The *Brahmin* was his mouth, of both his arms was the *Kshatriya* made. His thighs became the *Vaisya*; from his feet the *Sudra* was produced (*Rig-Veda*, 10.90.11–12).

The myth of the division of Purusha's body tells of the sacred origin of the classes of Hindu society. To live within one's class, to do one's duty as a member of that class is to follow the moral 'ought', the Hindu *dharma*. To fail to abide by one's social class makes one an 'outcaste', one who ceases to live by the divinely prescribed order. This is why Joshi concludes that the caste system is 'not merely a social institution' but 'predominantly a religious institution' (1975, 72).

The examples cited above demonstrate that morality comes out of scripture and is thus connected to the hierophanies by myths which, as we have previously seen, convey their transforming power in the life of believers through ritual re-enactments. The moral teachings of a religion, therefore, are imperative for the religious community if it is to remain in the sacred, in the 'really real', and thus respond appropriately to what it conceives to be of unrestricted value.

The distinction between morality and ethics

In his book on the religious experience of mankind, Ninian Smart (1984, 19) defines one dimension of that experience as 'the ethical'. He says that 'ethics concerns the behaviour of the individual and, to some extent, the code of ethics of the dominant religion controls the community'. Smart seems to be using ethics in the same way we have used morality. The two terms can be used interchangeably but, for purposes of clarity, a distinction should be made.

Morality, as we have used it, refers to an 'ought' or imperative derived from a hierophany and communicated to the people through scripture (either oral or written). Ethics, on the other hand, analyses why an imperative actually is (or is not) an imperative. It establishes, therefore, theories which either justify or dispute the 'oughts' of a religious community.

When I refer to morality as a religious phenomenon, I am suggesting that its force is derived from what the believers regard as sacred and hence comes to them with an ultimate authority. Ethics does not accept the authority of the hierophany but exposes it to an academic analysis. The end of this procedure might result in a moral imperative, but it will be one which has been derived not from a sacred event, but from analytical thinking.

Believers may use the tools of ethics to justify what they already regard as a moral imperative. This is a form of apologetics, theological arguments created to support what has previously been accepted on other grounds. Morality thus constitutes a part of religious phenomena since it is derived from the believing community's response to the sacred. Ethical analysis comes from this source only secondarily (in the form of apologetics) and does not require that one be a believer to engage in it. Ethics, therefore, as I have defined it, does not form a part of religious phenomena. Table 7.1 demonstrates this relationship.

Table 7.1

THE RELATIONSHIP BETWEEN MORALITY AND ETHICS

Morality	*Ethics*
The 'ought' is revealed.	The 'ought' is analysed.
The 'ought' is obeyed.	The 'ought' is followed for the reasons suggested in the analysis.
The 'ought' is not questioned.	The 'ought' is open to challenge.
Disobedience produces chaos.	The consequences of the failure to follow the 'ought' depend on the analysis.
The sacred 'ought' defines the primary concern as how a believer is to live.	The 'ought' concerns a believer only secondarily as apologetics.
Part of religious phenomena.	Excluded from the phenomena.

Summary

Scripture and morality demonstrate two further interrelationships among religious phenomena. We have also seen in our examination of the process whereby scripture and morality develop that a close connection exists between them and that myths and rituals form part of the oral tradition. Moreover, as we have previously observed, sacred practitioners and art-forms closely relate to myths and rituals and thus, by applying our current analysis, we can see how they might be connected to scripture and morality. Our discussion of myths, rituals, sacred practitioners, art, scripture and morality, therefore, suggests that the processes and interrelationships among all of the phenomena are complex and that other combinations could also have been profitably analysed.

The particular combinations we have discussed in the previous three chapters have been selected for the purpose of seeing into the meaning of each classification and to demonstrate that no classification operates in isolation from the others. We now conclude our discussion of the phenomenological categories by considering the special case of belief as a classification uniquely related to all of the others.

References

ALI, A. Y. (trans. and commentator).   1977   *The Glorious Qur'ān* (n.p., Muslim Students' Association of the United States and Canada).

COWARD, H.   1988   *Sacred Word and Sacred Text* (Maryknoll, Orbis).

GRAHAM, A. C.   1959   'Confucianism', in R. C. Zaehner (ed.), *Concise Encyclopaedia of Living Faiths* (Boston, Beacon), 365–84 .

JOSHI, L. M.   1975   'The caste system in India', in G. S. Talib (ed.), *The Origin and Development of Religion* (Patiala, Punjab Univ.), 64–77.

KRAMER, K.   1986   *World Scriptures: An Introduction to Comparative Religion* (New York, Paulist Press).

RAY, B. C.   1976   *African Religions* (Englewood Cliffs, Prentice-Hall).

SMART, N.   1984   *The Religious Experience of Mankind* (Glasgow, Collins).

Questions and Activities

Questions for discussion

1. Do you think the oral traditions hold a higher or more prominent place than the written texts among religious communities? Why or why not?

2. Give an example of how a biblical hierophany led to an oral tradition which was later recorded.

3. 'African religions are pre-literate and thus inferior to religions with written scriptures.' Discuss this statement.

4. List the reasons offered in this chapter as to why oral traditions have been recorded. Evaluate each of the reasons. Suggest others that might apply.

5. Write down an 'ought' which governs your life. Would you call your 'ought' morality or ethics? Why or why not?

6. Why does this chapter exclude ethics from religious phenomena?

Projects and activities

1. Read a selection silently from a written scripture of your choice. Then ask someone to read it aloud to you. Record your emotions in response to both the reading silently and aloud (for example, felt joyful, angry, hurt, indifferent, confused, and so on). Which had a more powerful effect on you, the written or the oral presentation?

2. Compare and contrast the quotation in this chapter from Confucius concerning the moral 'ought' with the Ten Commandments of the Hebrew tradition. Write a five-page essay incorporating your observations.

3. Keep a journal for one week in which you write at the end of each day how well you observed your own 'ought' which governs your life. Would you call your 'ought' morality or ethics? Indicate where you think you succeeded and where you failed. Then record what you will do about your failures. After the week has passed, read your journal. Are your responses basically 'religious?' Is your analysis consistent with your answer to the previous question?

Chapter Eight
The Special Case of Belief

So far in this book we have not considered beliefs as religious phenomena nor have we related them to other phenomena. This is because beliefs hold a unique place within religious experience and thus constitute a special case in the study of religious phenomena. They also hold a unique position in relation to the sacred dimension.

Because we have been building the paradigm of religion from below, beginning with the phenomena themselves, we have not yet examined the object of the religious person's concern or how he attains a perception of it. An examination of beliefs will guide us in that direction. At the conclusion of our discussion of beliefs, we will still need to examine important distinctions within the sacred dimension, but, because we are approaching the subject beginning with the phenomena and building towards understanding, we continue to use the terms unrestricted value and the sacred interchangeably and uncritically, as we have throughout this book.

What are beliefs?

Whenever an adherent of a religious tradition articulates to himself or to others what the unrestricted value is, he uses beliefs. To do this he must think something about the sacred. That thinking comprises a belief. Beliefs, therefore, can be defined as *thoughts, ideas or opinions about what people respond to as being of unrestricted value for them.*

If, for example, a person were to ask an adherent to explain his unrestricted value, the adherent would use an idea or thought to express his meaning. The thought or idea employs words for the sake of understanding and communication. The unrestricted value is not identical with the belief expressed in the words, but the belief helps the adherent himself understand the meaning of his unrestricted value and assists him to communicate it to others.

The relationship of beliefs to other phenomena and to the sacred

Beliefs are contained within each of the phenomenological classifications. They may not always be stated explicitly, but beliefs can be derived from these classifications. The believer has some idea of the sacred when he hears the myths recited or participates in their ritual re-enactment. He observes a sacred practitioner and understands something about what is being mediated. The believer may experience the unrestricted value directly through an icon or enter into an ecstatic emotional state under the influence of dancing and drumming, but he will still have an idea of what constitutes the object of the icon or into what sacred dimension he is entering through his state of ecstasy. In hearing the reading of scriptures, the believer will recognize pointers towards the unrestricted value and its moral authority over him. The phenomenologist enters into these phenomena, names them, and then seeks to determine from them *what* the believers hold about the sacred.

With these relationships in mind, we are now ready to portray the paradigmatic model which constitutes step 7 in the phenomenological model. Figure 8.1 illustrates the relationships between beliefs and other phenomena and beliefs and the sacred dimension.

This model describes how a believing community experiences the sacred through the phenomena containing the beliefs which define for that community what the unrestricted value actually is.

Although the relationship between the believer and the sacred dimension is depicted in Figure 8.1 as moving in a single direction, it actually involves a two-way process. The individual in the community (the I–We) not only enters into an experience of the sacred through the beliefs found in the phenomena but also interprets and communicates that experience through them. Whatever experience has occurred, therefore, will include a cognitive aspect without which the experience cannot be comprehended by the believer, the believing community or those outside the community.

This entering into an experience of the sacred from the phenomena through beliefs and a return through beliefs to the phenomena demonstrates the cycle of religious experience, which is depicted in Figure 8.2.

Types of beliefs

Beliefs primarily define what religious traditions think about the nature of the sacred. But they also define what the traditions hold about the human relationship to the sacred. That relationship almost always entails a fundamental human predicament which needs resolving and hence creates a further category of beliefs dealing with salvation. The three main types of beliefs which operate within the phenomena are, therefore: the *numinological,* which defines the unrestricted value; the *anthropological,* which focuses on the human (including the world in which the human lives); and the *soteriological,* which deals with the way in which the human achieves salvation.

The three types of beliefs follow one another in a descending order. The numinological belief determines the other two since the anthropological is derived from the numinological and the soteriological is obtained from the

Figure 8.1: THE PARADIGMATIC MODEL

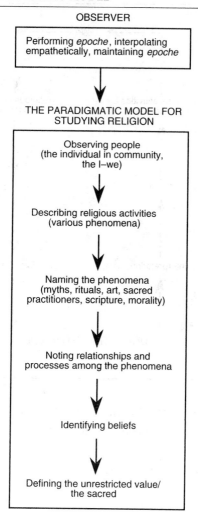

OBSERVER

Performing *epoche*, interpolating
empathetically, maintaining *epoche*

THE PARADIGMATIC MODEL FOR
STUDYING RELIGION

Observing people
(the individual in community,
the I–we)

Describing religious activities
(various phenomena)

Naming the phenomena
(myths, rituals, art, sacred
practitioners, scripture, morality)

Noting relationships and
processes among the phenomena

Identifying beliefs

Defining the unrestricted value/
the sacred

numinological through the anthropological. The self's response to the unrestricted value, therefore, is determined by the soteriological belief which defines the central human problem in relation to the sacred. A simple outline of these relationships is presented in Figure 8.3.

We now look in detail at the numinological, anthropological and soteriological beliefs as exemplified within the Vedantic form of Hinduism which will help us understand these types of belief and how they are interrelated.

Figure 8.2:   THE CYCLE OF RELIGIOUS EXPERIENCE

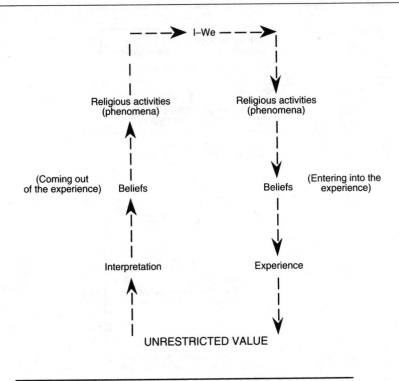

Figure 8.3:   THE RELATIONSHIP BETWEEN NUMINOLOGICAL, ANTHROPO-
LOGICAL AND SOTERIOLOGICAL BELIEFS

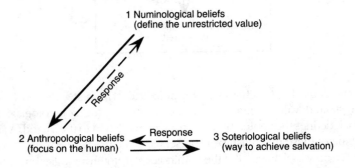

The types of beliefs within Vedantic Hinduism

Vedantic forms of Hinduism provide us with an excellent example of how the numinological, anthropological and soteriological beliefs interrelate within a religious tradition. Vedanta literally means 'end of the Veda' and refers to a philosophic type of Hinduism which emerged around the sixth century BCE (before the Common Era). The Vedas are the authoritative written scriptures for all forms of Hinduism. The literature within the Vedas is lengthy and developed over the 1 000 years after the Aryan peoples moved, in successive waves, from central Asia into the Indus valley some time about 2000 BCE.

The Veda are divided into four books called the *Rig-Veda, Sama Veda, Yajur Veda* and *Atharva Veda*. Each of these contains various types of writings: hymns to the gods and rituals, called the *Brahmanas*; interpretations of the rituals, the *Aranyakas*; and at the end of each Veda philosophical speculations, called the *Upanishads*, which were written between 800 and 500 BCE. It is on the *Upanishads* that Vedantic philosophy is based.

The *Upanishads* ask fundamental questions about life. The word *Upanishads* translated from Sanskrit means 'sitting down near' and may refer to the Indian tradition of putting oneself under the guidance of a teacher (*guru*). This would mean that the *Upanishads* are the source of wisdom and that one needs to 'sit down near' them, meditate on them, and learn about the nature of reality, oneself and one's ultimate destiny from them. There are about two hundred *Upanishads*, but, as the tradition has developed, eighteen are now considered authoritative.

Another form of literature about the *Upanishads* are the *Sutras*. The most important of these for Vedantic thinking are the *Brahma Sutras* which function as guides to the meaning of the *Upanishads* themselves. They were probably composed in the second century BCE. They contain short comments called aphorisms which are often difficult to understand. The reader of the *Brahma Sutras* needs to study each aphorism over and over in deep meditation to arrive at understanding (Klostermaier, 1989, 61–73; Kramer, 1986, 18-30; Smart, 1989, 50–6, 71–4).

Because of their cryptic content, the *Brahma Sutras* themselves required a commentary or interpretation. Three main writers on the Vedantic philosophy emerged between the eighth and the thirteenth centuries CE, each offering an interpretation of the *Upanishads* often based on the *Brahma Sutras*. The three are Sankara (778–820 CE), Madhva (*c.* 1230 CE) and Ramanuja (died 1127 CE). These three developed different theories about the nature of the ultimate and the relationship of the human and the world to it (Copleston, 1982, 68–95; Hinnells and Sharpe, 1972, 49–51). In our discussion of the Vedantic philosophy, we will follow the *Upanishads* as they came through the non-dualist interpretation of Sankara.

Within Vedantic thinking, the ultimate or unrestricted value is called *Brahman*. *Brahman* must first be understood as transcendent or beyond the human and the world in which the human lives. *Brahman* is thus described in the *Katha Upanishad* as immortal, the source of all things, that from which the whole universe emerged, the 'Primal Cause'. These terms would seem to emphasize the absolute 'otherness' of the unrestricted value from the human.

It is here, however, that the immanence (nearness to the human) of *Brahman* is revealed, since *Brahman* is found in and actually is identical with the true Self in each person, the *Atman*. The *Atman* is described in the *Katha Upanishad* (I, 2, 18, translated by Radhakrishnan, 1974, 616) in terms of what could only be ascribed to *Brahman*. 'The . . . Self . . . is never born; nor does he die at any time. He sprang from nothing and nothing sprang from him. He is unborn, eternal, abiding and primeval'. The Self is *Brahman*; *Brahman* is the Self.

This *Brahman–Atman* unity defines the central numinological belief within Vedantic Hinduism. It is summarized in the Sanskrit phrase '*tat tvam asî*', translated into English as 'that thou art'. Its meaning is explained in the *Chandogya Upanishad* (VI, 13, 3): 'Though you do not see *Brahman* in this body, he is indeed here. That which is the subtle essence — in that have all things their existence. That is the truth. That is the Self [*Atman*]. And that . . . thou art [*tat tvam asî*].'

Although *Brahman* seems to be spoken of here in personal terms, as Vedantic philosophy was interpreted through Sankara, *Brahman* is referred to more as a universal 'world spirit', the only true reality encompassing all things. '*Tat tvam asî*' suggests that this world spirit, the only true reality, is identical with the true Self found within every self. Frederick Copleston summarizes this belief: '*Brahman* is the sole reality and the permanent element in you is not different from *Brahman*' (1982, 77).

Closely related to this numinological belief is the Vedantic anthropological belief, the teaching about the nature of the self. This teaching emerges from the question about the exact relationship between each individual self and the universal world spirit. That question has been posed by Eric Lott (1980, 38): 'If the transcendent SELF alone is the ultimate reality, how can any finite being share its nature?'

The first answer to this is suggested by Lott himself (p. 39), who warns against confusing what he calls the 'empirical ego' with the *Atman*. The empirical ego refers to what each of us calls our 'self': our individual personalities, our bodies, our feelings and our emotional states. Yet this empirical ego is not unborn, not eternal, not the source of the entire universe. This self will change, decay and ultimately die. It cannot be the *Brahman*; it cannot be the true Self.

This distinction between the empirical ego and the true inner Self is underscored by the story of the visit of the god Indra and the demon

Virochana to the famous teacher Prajapati as related in the *Chandogya Upanishad* (VIII, 7–12). After sitting with Prajapati for thirty-two years, Indra and Virochana define what they want to learn: 'We have heard . . . that one who realizes the Self obtains all the worlds and all desires. We have lived here because we want to learn of this Self.'

Prajapati responds by telling the two enquirers to look into a pool of water and report what they see. They return and tell him that they have seen their bodies. Then Prajapati instructs them to put on their finest clothes and look again. This time when asked what they have seen, Indra and Virochana answer, 'We have seen the Self; we have seen even the hair and the nails'. Prajapati concurs that it is true that indeed they have seen the Self.

Virochana goes back to the land of the demons well pleased that he has understood Prajapati's teaching correctly that the body is the Self. The *Chandogya Upanishad* comments, 'Such doctrine is, in very truth, the doctrine of the demons!' But Indra realizes before ever arriving back in the land of the gods that he had not understood the meaning of the lesson. He therefore returns to Prajapati for another thirty-two years. At the conclusion of this long period, Indra reports to have learned the following: 'That which moves about in dreams, enjoying sensuous delight and clothed in glory, that is the Self. That is immortal, that is fearless, and that is *Brahman*.'

What Indra had learned was that a part of each individual self can be detached from the body. That is the self known in dreams. If one is blind in the body, for example, the self can see in dreams. If one is lame in the body, in dreams one can run and leap. With this knowledge, Indra believed that he had learned the secret of the true Self and headed back to the land of the gods.

Before arriving to share his insight with the gods, however, Indra realized that this knowledge also was deficient since even in dreams the self 'is conscious of many sufferings'. Every person knows the terror of dreams, the disappointments of dreams, the anger of dreams. This, therefore, cannot be the pure bliss of the unchanging, eternal Self. Once again Indra went back to Prajapati for further teaching.

Indra then describes the third lesson he obtained from Prajapati after the conclusion of another thirty-two years of instruction. 'When a man is sound asleep, free from dreams and at perfect rest — that is the Self. The Self is immortal and fearless, and it is *Brahman*.' The true Self thus is like a dreamless sleep, undisturbed by any outside forces, free from suffering and in a state of perfect peace. This deeper understanding had pushed Indra towards an apprehension of the *Atman*; but he was bothered by one further problem. Surely this dreamless state is like being unconscious where one is aware of nothing. He ponders that this must be 'next to annihilation' and returns to Prajapati for help.

Indra's final stay with Prajapati lasts only five years until he discovers the true meaning of the Self. From his first thirty-two years he had learned that 'this body is mortal, always gripped by death, but within it dwells the immortal Self'. After his second thirty-two years he learned that the inner self 'when associated in our consciousness with the body' continues to be subjected to pleasure and pain. His third period taught him that, as the association of the consciousness with the body ceases, there also cease pleasure and pain. His last five years taught him the final insight whereby he could connect these three truths: the concern with annihilation becomes a problem only so long as a person persists in associating the state of consciousness which is like a dreamless sleep with individual bodily existence.

This latter point needs further explanation. When a person is in a deep sleep, he cannot be said to be unconscious; otherwise, how could he awaken and feel renewed physically and mentally? After a deep, dreamless sleep, he says something like, 'I slept so well. I feel so refreshed.' He is even able to think back to his peace and know that he had slept well. But while in this condition he was not aware of being an individual connected to a personal body. It was as if he had experienced a consciousness beyond physical consciousness.

This type of consciousness is like discovering the true Self (*Atman*) and apprehending its unity with *Brahman*. Dreamless sleep is analogous to experiencing the absorption of individual consciousness into universal Consciousness. Indra concludes: 'Rising above physical consciousness, knowing the Self to be distinct from the senses and the mind — knowing it in its true light — one rejoices and is free.'

The story of Indra and Prajapati leads us to the central Vedantic conclusion about the self. The idea that the empirical ego is the true Self is an illusion and results from what Sankara called 'wrong conception' (Lott, 1980, 45). The deepest Self is fundamentally different from the empirical ego because it is Pure Consciousness, *Brahman*. The anthropological belief of Vedantic thinking, therefore, is that the physical self which people take to be real is an illusion. The self which is real is the eternal *Brahman* freed from physical existence, individual consciousness and the ignorance which results from associating the two together.

This anthropological belief leads towards the Vedantist's description of the human predicament and thus defines what constitutes his central soteriological belief. The fundamental human problem in Vedantic thinking is ignorance, mistaking the unreal for the real and failing to comprehend what is really real. This ignorance has the effect of maintaining the cycle of birth and re-birth (the transmigration of souls or reincarnation) according to the law of *karma*. If one overcomes ignorance and sees into reality, the karmic cycle will be broken and no transmigration of souls will occur. We need to explain karma and transmigration briefly, therefore, to understand the Vedantic teaching on salvation.

The law of karma is held throughout the many forms of Hinduism. It defines life in terms of moral causes and effects. In its most strict interpretation, it holds that every deed which a person commits, for good or evil, will result in an appropriate reward or punishment. Everything a person experiences in this life, therefore, is deserved; everything a person does in this life will produce a just effect (Klostermaier, 1989, 204–6).

Clearly, this law cannot operate within one life. People do not always receive appropriate rewards or punishments according to their actions in this life. For this reason, karma must be accompanied by the idea of the transmigration of souls. The self must 'migrate across' one life into another life and be born again in another body. The rewards one deserves in the present life, therefore, may be experienced in future lives or the rewards one is experiencing in this life may have been earned in previous lives. Likewise, the penalties one deserves for bad conduct may not be experienced until future lives or the sufferings one experiences in this life may be caused by evil behaviour in previous lives.

The law of karma and its related theory of the transmigration of souls construct a universe based on an absolute system of cosmic justice. There is no innocent suffering. Everything one experiences for good or for evil is experienced in exact proportion to previous deeds (Cox, 1989, 17–18).

Although this belief constructs a judicial order, it proposes two things which are objectionable within Vedantic thinking: it confuses pleasure and pain in bodily existence with reality; and it perpetuates an endless cycle of birth and re-birth, keeping the Self eternally bound within physical existence and preventing it from achieving unity with *Brahman*.

The first Vedantic objection is clear. Reward or punishment are associated with pleasure or pain in the physical existence, including the particular caste within Indian society into which one is born. Caste is determined by the law of karma and carried out at birth through appropriate transmigrations of the soul. Those in the lowest, menial positions in society should perform their duties faithfully according to the law of karma in order that they might be born into a higher station in the next life and thus minimize their suffering. In Vedantic thought, however, the body is always subject to pain and can never attain eternal pleasure.

The second Vedantic objection to karma and transmigration is based on the first problem. If karma and transmigration are real, the Self will be re-born endlessly into various states of physical existence and hence will be bound not only to suffering but to separation from the source and ground of all existence, the eternal *Brahman*. Humanity, therefore, will never achieve its true purpose and meaning so long as it remains enslaved to the laws of karma and the transmigration of souls.

The Self, therefore, needs to be released or liberated from the endless cycle of birth and re-birth and find its unity with *Brahman*. This liberation is called *moksha* and defines the Vedantic soteriological belief. The cause of the continued enslavement to karma and transmigration is ignorance. The person must come to see the whole system as *maya*, illusion. When this occurs, one no longer confuses the individual empirical ego with the true inner Self and so one is able to be freed from ignorance into the pure bliss of the *Brahman–Atman* unity. That is moksha, release from the illusion of karma and the transmigration of souls, from the illusion that the true Self is subject to these laws, from the illusion that the Self is tied to the body. To be released is to be saved.

The Hindu scholar, K. Sivaraman (1974, 4–5), likens moksha to waking up from a dream where the dreamer has taken his illusion for reality. Sivaraman suggests that this waking up is 'a possibility always, at any given time *but at no particular time*'. Since karma and transmigration of souls are illusions, they persist so long as people continue to take them to be real. The awakening can occur at any time at all, but it is not a time within history. Rather, it is a release from the illusion of history into the eternal *Brahman*.

We have now presented in a concise way the central Vedantic numino-logical, anthropological and soteriological beliefs. A summary of these beliefs follows:

Numinological: The unrestricted value is the eternal world spirit called *Brahman* and its unity with the true Self within all selves called the *Atman*.

Anthropological: The empirical ego (the body and the mind's connection to the body) is an illusion; the true Self is the *Atman*.

Soteriological: Salvation entails release (moksha) from illusion (which perpetuates the cycles of karma and transmigration of the soul) into the realization of the unity of the true Self with *Brahman*.

It will be clear from this summary that each type of belief is related to the other and that the numinological (the statement of what is of unrestricted value) determines the anthropological and the soteriological beliefs. Because the *Brahman–Atman* unity is the unrestricted value, the individual self is defined strictly in terms of the universal Self, ignorance of which creates the need for salvation.

Deriving the beliefs from the phenomena

We have derived the Vedantic numinological, anthropological and soteriological beliefs largely from the phenomenon of scripture. We have referred to the *Upanishads* and their interpretations by classical Vedantic scholars. The particular sections of the *Upanishads* to which we referred contained a story as an art form in order to illustrate the belief. But primarily these beliefs have been obtained from the phenomenon of written scriptures.

The same beliefs can be derived from a particular ritual practiced widely within Vedantic meditation. This involves uttering the sacred sound 'OM'. This can be done in a group, in relation to a *guru*, or alone. The sound is given to help the adherent experience, in Sivaraman's words (1974, 5), that 'you and I differ in our bodies, in the minds and egos associated with bodies, but we do not differ in self'.

'OM' actually consists of three letters corresponding in English to A-U-M. They represent the three levels of consciousness attained by Indra through his patient study under Prajapati. The first letter represents the fact that the body is not the same as the Self but that in the body dwells the immortal Self. This represents the first level of meditation as the person goes deeper into his true Self. The U stands for the second level of awareness that the Self is not identical with the individual consciousness attached to a body, but that within each consciousness resides the immortal Self. The M is the recognition that the true Self is the Pure Consciousness of the immortal *Brahman*, without either individuality or annihilation, apprehended by rising above the physical senses and the mind (Kramer, 1986, 27–8).

As the Vedantist utters the sound, he goes from the first through the second to the third level of awareness through a process of meditation and concentration. When this is done in groups, the leader may ask the adherents to close their eyes, imagine a line of connection between all the persons in the group, and then to utter the sacred sound in unison. The result is a resonating, deep vibration in which individuality is overcome in the unity of the group on the horizontal level and each empirical ego in the vertical dimension goes deeply through the meditation to discover the true Self within all selves.

OM represents in an experiential way a process of discovering the *Brahman–Atman* unity, the illusion of the empirical ego and the release from ignorance into the pure consciousness of the *Brahman–Atman*. This ritual of meditation therefore contains within it the very same numinological, anthropological and soteriological beliefs which were derived from the *Upanishads*.

Why beliefs form a special case in religious phenomena

This survey of beliefs within the phenomena of Vedantic Hinduism exemplifies the special case of beliefs within religious traditions. The Vedantist enters into an experience of the unrestricted value through his belief that his individual self is an illusion and that to be saved he must grasp the meaning of the unity of his true inner Self with the ultimate world spirit. Once he has experienced this unity, he understands its meaning in terms of beliefs. If he seeks to communicate this, he will use the same beliefs to help others into a similar relationship with what he has conceived to be and experienced as the unrestricted value.

This entering into an experience of the unrestricted value will not always be achieved using the words of belief but may be accomplished through rituals, mythic re-enactments, through the mediation of a sacred practitioner, within art, or by a hearing or reading of scripture. But the beliefs will still be present within these phenomena and thus will perform a necessary function in defining and interpreting religious experience.

The need to compare beliefs

Although the paradigm for beliefs as derived from and returning to the phenomena is the same within all religious traditions, the content of beliefs varies across the traditions. *What* religions believe about the sacred, about the human and about salvation is not the same. By carefully studying the phenomena, therefore, the phenomenologist is able to use the tools of *epochē* and empathetic interpolation to derive beliefs which can be compared both in terms of their common instrumental functions and their distinctive contents.

The various religious traditions, therefore, can be compared according to the paradigmatic model and the cycle of religious experience we have diagrammed earlier. We follow the phenomenological steps to arrive at a description of myths, rituals, sacred practitioners, art, scripture and morality within any one tradition, out of which we define its numinological, anthropological and soteriological beliefs. We can then label these beliefs as the religious structure of a particular tradition, do the same for any other tradition, and compare them accordingly. The comparison of religious beliefs within the phenomenological method is shown in Figure 8.4.

By insisting on using the phenomenological method in the derivation of beliefs, the student of religion is able to avoid defining the beliefs of one religion in terms of another. It is not possible, for example, to take the Hindu idea of *avatara* (the appearances of the divine in animal, animal–human and human forms) and evaluate it as a lower illustration of the Christian belief about the incarnation of Jesus if one understands that these two beliefs are quite distinct in relation to the myths, rituals, sacred practitioners and other phenomena within each tradition.

The phenomenological approach also prevents beliefs from being presented merely as abstract concepts unrelated to religious phenomena. The student, therefore, is warned against simply comparing a type of belief within one religion with a similar type in another as if they were merely intellectual concepts unrelated to the phenomena themselves.

These comparisons of beliefs within the traditions, however, are

Figure 8.4: HOW TO COMPARE RELIGIOUS BELIEFS WITHIN THE PHENOMENO-
LOGICAL METHOD

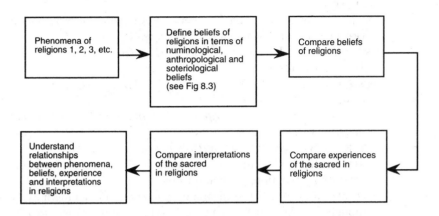

undertaken for the specific purpose of gaining understanding through the phenomenological process. Not only do they enable the phenomenologist to achieve an understanding of particular religions but they inform his effort to see into the meaning of religion itself — the eidetic intuition. To accomplish this requires the comparison between the beliefs of different religions, but only after a careful application of the phenomenological stages.

We will return to the eidetic intuition in the last chapter. Before we can complete the phenomenological process, however, we must take the next logical step from identifying beliefs to considering the unrestricted value and the sacred. Although the special case of belief has helped us understand the instrumental relationship of beliefs to the sacred within religious traditions, we have seen that beliefs are not perceived by those traditions as being identical with the sacred. We need to examine the object of belief, therefore, before we can move towards a broad interpretation of the meaning of religion in general.

References

COPLESTON, F. 1982 *Religion and the One* (New York, Crossroad Publications).

COX, J. L. 1989 'Karma and redemption: A religious approach to family violence', *Journal of Religion and Health*, XXVIII, 16–25.

HINNELLS, J. R. and E. J. SHARPE (eds.) 1972 *Hinduism* (Newcastle upon Tyne, Oriel Press).

KLOSTERMAIER, K. K. 1989 *A Survey of Hinduism* (Albany, State Univ. of New York).

KRAMER, K. 1986 *World Scriptures. An Introduction to Comparative Religions* (New York, Paulist Press).

LOTT, E. 1980 *Vedantic Approaches to God* (London, Macmillan).

RADHAKRISHNAN, S. (trans. and commentator) 1974 *The Principal Upanishads* (London, Allen and Unwin).

SIVARAMAN, K. 1974 'The meaning of *moksha* in contemporary Hindu thought and life', in S. J. Samartha (ed.), *Living Faiths and Ultimate Goals* (Maryknoll, Orbis Books), 2–11.

SMART, N. 1989 *The World's Religions: Old Traditions and Modern Transformations* (Cambridge, Cambridge Univ. Press).

Questions and Activities

Questions for discussion

1. Discuss how beliefs are contained in a) myths; b) rituals; c) sacred practitioners; d) art; e) scripture; and f) morality. What does your discussion tell you about the author's argument regarding belief as a 'special case' in the phenomena of religion?

2. Do you agree that anthropological and soteriological beliefs are derived from numinological beliefs? Why or why not? If not, give examples of numinological beliefs which have been obtained from anthropological and/or soteriological beliefs.

3. How could '*tat tvam asi*' be numinological, anthropological and soteriological at the same time?

4. What is meant by dreamless sleep? Could one be conscious and later not recall being conscious?

5. Study the cycle of religious experience shown in Figure 8.2. Describe the function of beliefs according to this diagram.

Projects and activities

1. List the fundamental beliefs you hold personally. Answer the following questions for each:
   a) In what myths do I find this belief?
   b) How do I experience it in rituals?
   c) How does the belief relate to sacred practitioners?
   d) What art expresses it?
   e) Where do I find it in scriptures?
   f) Does it lead to moral behaviour?
2. Find a person to talk to. Ask that person to share his/her religious experience with you. (Be sure the person is speaking of an experience.) Afterwards, record on paper the beliefs through which the person entered the experience and through which he/she interpreted it to you.
3. Meditate on the Hindu OM for 60 minutes by doing the following: a) find a quiet place to be alone; b) read the story of Virochana and Prajapati again; c) meditate on the reading and then try to move deeply into your own inner consciousness by applying the A-U-M steps. After the exercise, indicate how well you think you succeeded in the meditation. What obstacles stood in your way? Were any of these obstacles related to your own beliefs?

PART III

Towards the Meaning of Religion

Chapter Nine
The Sacred and the Unrestricted Value

Professor Andrew Walls of Edinburgh is fond of saying to his students that, according to the phenomenological method, 'God is not a part of the phenomena'. In a way he is right, since maintaining *epoché* means that the phenomenologist brackets out or suspends all judgements concerning the truth claims of any religion. Nevertheless, the unrestricted value, by definition, is the most important aspect of the phenomena. In this chapter we consider the unrestricted value in the light of faith and an enlarged meaning of the sacred. In the process, we are led to qualify some of our previous definitions of the phenomenological categories and come to a conclusion regarding the structure of religion according to this method.

The unrestricted value as the focus of faith

Ninian Smart (1973, 62) defines the object towards which the phenomena point by the term 'focus of faith'. Smart argues that each religious tradition expresses 'faith in the focus . . . of that tradition'. He thus includes three aspects within his analysis of religious affirmation: expressions, faith and focus.

Expressions

Smart defines the expressions of faith as the doctrinal, the mythic and the ethical dimensions of a religious tradition. The doctrinal refers to what we have called beliefs; the mythic includes the sacred stories, ritual re-enactments of them, often sacred practitioners and art; the ethical is the equivalent of what we have called morality derived from scripture. The expressions of the focus, therefore, are equivalent to the phenomena.

Faith

By referring to the phenomena as expressions of the focus of faith, Smart is drawing a distinction between faith and the phenomena themselves. Faith represents the human apprehension of the sacred which is able to recognize its manifestations. In other words, faith perceives the hierophany (to use Eliade's term) as a hierophany. The manifestation becomes an appearance of the sacred only for the faithful who then express their faith through the phenomena. Smart implies, therefore, that faith is an organ for perceiving the unrestricted value.

Focus

Smart says the 'focus' is what the tradition's 'ideas and practices refer to or are directed at' (p. 63). It is the unrestricted value. The term focus suggests an analogy to the image visible through the lens of a camera. To be 'in focus' is to bring the object directly and clearly before the observer. To be 'out of focus' is to present a blurred image through the lens. Smart's 'focus of faith', then, refers to what the adherent sees clearly by faith through its manifestations expressed in the phenomena.

If we follow Smart, we must conclude that faith stands between the focus (unrestricted value) and the phenomena which contain beliefs about the focus. This suggests that our figure of the structure of religion presented in the last chapter (Figure 8.1) remains incomplete without the addition of faith as a separate category (see Figure 9.1) This demonstrates that faith holds a special place in the model between the unrestricted value and beliefs. To understand the meaning of the unrestricted value within the structure of religion, therefore, we need to examine the relationship between faith and beliefs.

The distinction between faith and beliefs

We suggested in the last chapter that beliefs define *what* a tradition thinks about the unrestricted value. Faith cannot be equated to those thoughts but it cannot be achieved nor interpreted without them. Beliefs, therefore, express the cognitive meaning of what faith has apprehended, but it is faith which has done the apprehending.

The Indian scholar D. G. Moses devoted much of his writing earlier this century to clarifying the distinction between faith and belief. He argued (1939, 72) that in any type of perception, although the object remains independent from the person who is doing the perceiving, the person always inserts himself into the act of perception and thus influences what is actually perceived. Moses contended that this is especially true with the object of religious perception which is not merely comprehended by the believer's intellect but also by his emotions.

Moses called this comprehensive involvement of the subject in the perception of the religious object 'integral knowing', a type of knowing which is equivalent to faith (Cox, 1980, 67). Moses (1954, 150) thus arrived at his definition of faith as 'the knowing capacity of man exercising itself in a certain comprehensiveness of outlook, taking into consideration the many-sidedness of the relation of the known reality to the knowing subject'. For Moses, therefore, faith is the *knowing capacity of man* directed towards what he has *comprehended in relation to the sacred* and hence what he *knows* to be real.

Figure 9.1: REVISED PARADIGMATIC MODEL

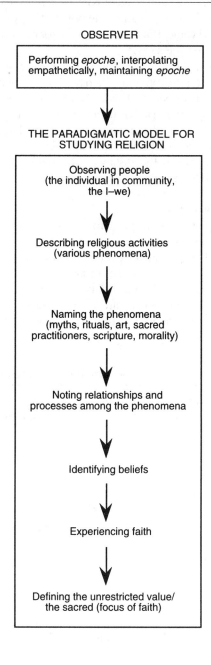

A knowing capacity can be distinguished from *what* is known. The capacity is empty in itself, void of content. Once the capacity is exercised it perceives or sees or apprehends the object. The content is the object itself, the unrestricted value. But faith is an organ for perception, the lens whereby the believer 'sees' the sacred.

This helps us distinguish faith from beliefs. When the adherent moves towards the faith perception or when he describes what he has perceived in faith he always uses beliefs. This is like a person who goes on a safari to see a lion for the first time. He has been told lions exist. He believes they exist. He has seen photographs of them. As he is travelling through a game park his guide stops, looks through his binoculars and tells the person that he has spotted a lion in the distance. The person then looks through the binoculars and 'sees' a lion for the first time in his life. He 'experiences' the object. When he returns home, he may relate to others excitedly *what* he saw directly 'with his own eyes'.

Beliefs form the starting point for the act of faith and they are required to interpret its content. But beliefs are not the same as the act of perceiving, nor are they identical with the content of faith. The content is the unrestricted value, what Smart calls the focus of faith; faith is the capacity for knowing the unrestricted value; beliefs are thoughts or ideas about the content and thus, again following Smart, are expressions of the focus. Faith can be known only in experience and thus remains the exclusive possession of the one who acts on it.

Implications for the phenomenological method

What an adherent within a religious tradition 'knows' in faith must be different from what the observer of that religious tradition knows. The observer, by definition, does not exercise faith. To do so would be to abandon *epoché* and embrace the tradition itself. This would eliminate the possibility of achieving objectivity and hence of attaining understanding of the meaning of religion.

The phenomenologist observes the phenomena, the expressions of the activity of faith. He can only describe the unrestricted value through beliefs which the adherent has used to enter the faith experience or to interpret it. By exercising *epoché* and empathetic interpolation, the phenomenologist may gain a 'feel for' the faith experience but he can never see directly into the focus itself through faith.

Wilfred Cantwell Smith (1978, 171) supports this view, arguing that the observer of any religious tradition must look at the expressions of faith in order to understand what faith is and what it has apprehended. Smith argues that faith is expressed in religious phenomena 'in words, both prose and poetry; in patterns of deeds, both ritual and morality; in art, in institutions, in law, in community; and in still many other ways'.

The expressions allow the phenomenologist, using his tools of *epochē* and empathetic interpolation, to 'see into' what actually cannot be seen without faith. Smith likens this to love, the uniquely personal meaning of which can be understood only by those who are or have been 'in love'. But an outsider can observe the expressions of love, the ways a person acts towards the one he loves and gain an understanding of what the person feels for his lover. In a similar way, the phenomenologist of religion observes the results of faith without actually exercising faith and thereby gains an understanding of what faith means for the believer.

The nature of the sacred

Having distinguished faith from beliefs and discussed its bearing on the phenomenological method, we are ready to move to an examination of the meaning of the unrestricted value. Two fundamental questions emerge from our discussion: Does faith perceive the sacred itself or its manifestations?, and Must the sacred actually exist for it to manifest itself? We address these two questions in the remainder of this chapter.

The sacred or its manifestations?

To answer whether faith perceives the sacred itself or the manifestations of the sacred, we review Mircea Eliade's definition of the hierophany or the sacred manifestation. Eliade (1959, 11) says that 'man becomes aware of the sacred because it manifests itself'. This 'becoming aware' corresponds to what we have defined as faith, namely, the act of perceiving the unrestricted value.

Eliade says that he means nothing more by the term hierophany than what the word implies, that is, '*that something sacred shows itself to us*' (his emphasis). Very simple hierophanies include particular stones or trees which stand out because they have become an object through which the sacred has appeared. An example of this is found in the Marondera region of Zimbabwe in a tree called '*muti usina zita*' (the tree without a name). This tree provides meat and sadza for those who perform rituals beneath it; it therefore constitutes a hierophany. Eliade says that sacred manifestations function in the same way for people in all religions including 'the supreme hierophany' for Christians which is the incarnation of Jesus Christ: 'In each case we are confronted by the same mysterious act — the manifestation of something of a wholly different order, a reality that does not belong to our world, in objects that are an integral part of our natural "profane" world' (1959, 11).

For Eliade, then, the sacred does not belong to our world but is made known in objects from stones to human beings which we know very well. These natural or 'profane' objects are not transformed into the sacred itself but become avenues for the appearance of the sacred. This implies that whatever the sacred is in reality always remains hidden to the human because it is something totally outside human experience. Objects through which the manifestations occur, however, are familiar, natural and commonplace. Faith can only 'see' the sacred through its manifestations. Beyond the manifestation lies another dimension: that of the mysterious, the unnamed and the indefinable.

If Eliade is correct, our previous use of the sacred as interchangeable with the unrestricted value and Smart's focus of faith has been mistaken. Both of these terms refer to the manifestation of the sacred and not to the sacred itself since the manifestation alone is comprehensible and capable of being expressed in the phenomena.

Because the sacred cannot be perceived directly nor interpreted apart from its manifestations, an insurmountable barrier is constructed between it and the other components of religious experience. The sacred acts through its manifestations, but only the manifestations are visible to the eyes of faith. This is why the focus of faith, that which is 'in clear view' for the believer, is not actually the sacred but its appearance in the world. The sacred remains unknown and unknowable.

An example of a religious tradition which directly embraces Eliade's distinction is the philosophic form of the Chinese religion called Taoism. In Taoist thinking, the Tao is the sacred, the 'way' of the universe, the final reality, the ineffable mystery, the ultimate. Many words are used to describe the Tao in Taoist scriptures: 'unchanging', 'moving everywhere, but never exhausted', 'the mother of all below heaven', the 'supreme'.

These words actually 'name' the Tao or bring it into human understanding through ideas, concepts or analogies. But one of the Taoist sacred writings called the *Tao Te Ching* distinguishes between this 'named' Tao and an 'unnamed Tao', the mystery which can never be named or expressed in words, thoughts or ideas. The opening lines of the *Tao Te Ching* (Part I, Chapter 1) elaborate on this point.

> If the Tao could be comprised in words, it would not be the unchangeable Tao;
> (For) if a name may be named, it is not an unchangeable name
>   (cited in Hughes, 1954, 144–5).

Behind its manifestations, the named Tao, stands the indefinable sacred mystery, the unnamed Tao.

Wilfred Cantwell Smith (1978, 186) also refers to something which stands behind or beyond faith and its expressions. Smith calls this the transcendent, but he means the same thing as Eliade's sacred and the Taoist's unnamed Tao. Smith argues that the transcendent 'is presumably the same for every man' and yet 'quite unknowable'. The workings of religion constitute a 'dialectical process between the mundane and the transcendent', the locus of which is 'personal faith'.

Just as the unnamed Tao cannot be named without its actually ceasing to be the Tao, the transcendent would cease to be totally other were it to be identical with its manifestations and expressions. The scholar of religion studies the manifestations and their expressions but cannot see beyond them. This is why Smith says the transcendent 'presumably' is the same for every person, but whether it is or not 'is not integral to our analysis'.

A re-thinking of numinological beliefs

In the last chapter, we defined numinological beliefs as thoughts about the sacred, defining its content in forms that the human mind can understand. If Eliade's distinction is correct, numinological beliefs are thoughts, not about the sacred itself, but about the manifestations of the sacred. This seems true in the case of Taoism where the manifestation is interpreted in human analogies such as causes, sources, birth, and even the flowing of water. The beliefs about the unnamed Tao can only be expressed in terms of the manifestations of the named Tao in human experience.

Let us look at another example, at what Eliade calls the 'supreme hierophany' for Christians, the incarnation of Jesus Christ. Christians believe they see in a human being what the sacred is like. They maintain, however, a distinction between the actual person who lived in first century Palestine and the sacred mystery itself. The writer of the Gospel of John refers to the 'Logos', an eternal word, the sacred reality. This Logos, which is the mystery behind all things, became flesh and dwelt in the person Jesus of Nazareth. We do not know the Logos itself, but we see its manifestation in Jesus who reveals the mystery in a way humans can understand and which is otherwise ineffable.

This example raises yet another question for our understanding of numinological beliefs. If beliefs describe the appearance of the sacred rather than the sacred itself, does 'God' refer to the sacred or to its manifestations? The answer here must be that, when God, like the named Tao, is given attributes such as creator, redeemer, sustainer, all-powerful or omniscient, God is actually being spoken of in terms of numinological beliefs. The beliefs express or interpret what the adherent has seen through faith as manifestations of a sacred mystery in the world. In Christian teaching, for example, people are able to look at the natural world and recognize that it manifests a creative act. When the creator is described, numinological beliefs appear. The looking at the world is the act of faith; but behind it all is an unnameable sacred entity about which nothing can be said apart from its manifestations. This unnameable mystery is not God, but that which stands beyond God. God is the manifestation, perceived by faith, interpreted in beliefs and expressed in the phenomena.

We find this same distinction in many other religious traditions. In Judaism, for example, YHWH (Yahweh) is a symbol for what cannot be named but can be apprehended through appearances in history. YHWH is simply the indescribable mystery, the 'I am that I am'. In Shona traditional religions of Zimbabwe, various terms are used to describe the sacred. One term is *dzivaguru* which translated means the 'big pool'; for the Shona, the sacred manifests itself in torrential rain. Beliefs can be formulated about this manifestation as they are expressed in myths and ritual actions, but behind *dzivaguru* stands an unknowable mystery.

This mystery behind all religions explains why numinological beliefs cannot be formulated about the sacred itself but only about its manifestations. Statements about the *Brahman–Atman* unity of Vedantic Hinduism, about the named Tao of Taoism, about *T'ien* in Confucianism, about Allah in Islam, about the God and Father of Jesus Christ in Christianity, or about *dzivaguru* in Shona traditional religion are all numinological beliefs about the manifestations of an ineffable sacred rather than the sacred itself.

This distinction leads to a further refinement in terms. The unrestricted value represents the *ultimate* manifestation of the sacred for any believing community as expressed through its numinological beliefs. As the supreme hierophany, therefore, the unrestricted value must be capable of manifesting itself. In other words, the ultimate manifestation for believers produces hierophanies of its own. In Islam, for example, Allah can be named or described only as a hierophany through perfected, but human-centred, attributes such as the all-knowing, all-beneficent and all-compassionate One. As the ultimate hierophany, however, Allah also manifests himself as he did to Muhammad through the Angel Gabriel. Islam recognizes this since it assigns ninety-nine names to Allah but reserves the hundredth name which cannot be reduced to human manifestations. This represents in the Islamic tradition what Eliade means by the unknown and unknowable sacred manifesting itself in a supreme hierophany (any tradition's unrestricted value) which then produces further manifestations of its own.

The sacred as a structure of the religious consciousness

The phenomenologist asks at this point if the distinction between the sacred and its manifestations represents the point of view of most adherents within religious traditions or if it has been superimposed on the phenomena by the scholar's own presuppositions. We have seen that religious people clearly recognize and name the manifestations, but do they all make a sharp demarcation between an ineffable mystery called the sacred and what they are able to perceive through faith as its manifestations?

Eliade (1969, Preface) answers this by suggesting that all religious people do make such a distinction because they possess an inner or subjective structure of consciousness through which they view reality. Because this is a subjective structure, Eliade 'intuits' its existence rather than observing it in the objective phenomena. The indescribable and unknowable sacred standing beyond its manifestations defines the necessary assumption within the structure of the *religious* consciousness, although that structure is not always overtly recognized by the believer.

This is similar to the working of our everyday consciousness whereby we perceive objects and their relations in the world. In order to make sense of the mind's perceptions, a structure which includes the category of causality must already be present within the human consciousness. If a person hears a door slam, for example, he associates the sound with the movement of the door and concludes that the noise was caused by the door moving rapidly toward its closed position. Prior to his coming to this conclusion, the observer must already have had the notion of cause and effect within his mind, a notion corresponding to the structure of how he perceives and understands the world. The person is not always aware that his idea of causality makes it possible for him to make associations among his various perceptions because the idea is already 'built into' his consciousness.

For the religious person, the sacred is 'built into' the structure of his consciousness; it defines the way he perceives and understands its manifestations. The phenomenologist is able to move through a study of the phenomena, beliefs and faith to describe what the adherent sees as the manifestations of the sacred, but he is able only to 'intuit' the sacred within the believer's religious consciousness. If this intuition is correct, however, every religious tradition points towards an unknowable sacred X which transcends all of its appearances within human experience (see Figure 9.2).

The idea of a religious consciousness helps us overcome the problem we referred to earlier that the observer does not and cannot possess faith and is thus subject to the charge that he cannot gain an understanding of any religious tradition from the believer's perspective. It is clear that the phenomenologist does not need to have faith in order to describe myths and rituals, sacred practitioners and art, scripture and morality and from them derive various types of beliefs. The intuition of the structure of religious consciousness means, however, that the phenomenologist need

Figure 9.2: THE STRUCTURE OF THE RELIGIOUS CONSCIOUSNESS

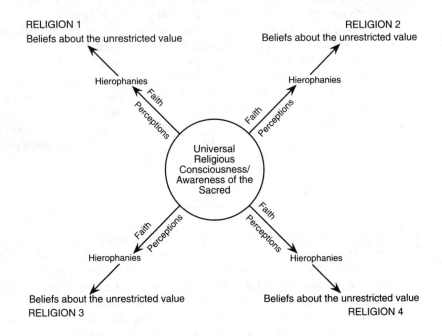

not 'know' what the sacred is in itself in order to describe what the adherents 'know' through faith to be its manifestations.

If we refer to the Christian example, we see that the phenomenologist does not need to possess faith to see the manifestation of the Logos, but he must perform *epochē* and maintain empathetic interpolation to understand the meaning of that manifestation for Christians. He is also able to point towards the indescribable in that which is describable (for Christians the incarnate Word) and intuit from this the operation of the sacred as a universal structure of religious consciousness.

The idea of a universal religious consciousness also helps resolve the problem of what phenomena should be included in or excluded from the study of religion which we discussed in the first chapter on the definitions of religion. Specifically, no ideology which fails to point towards the ineffable mystery (variously perceived in manifestations and defined in beliefs) can form a part of religious phenomena since the structure of the religious consciousness is lacking. This enables us to restrict the study of religion to those communities of believers which utilize faith as an organ for perceiving what those without faith could never see. All forms of humanism (Marxist, Freudian, utilitarian, etc.), therefore, must be excluded from the arena of religious studies in so far as they fail the essential test: to view the world through the religious mind.

Must the sacred exist in order to manifest itself?

Does the positing of an ineffable sacred behind all religious manifestations mean that the sacred exists in reality? Has Eliade's distinction, therefore, inadvertently pushed us from phenomenology into theology? The answer to this is implied in the idea of the 'structure of religious consciousness' which states nothing at all about things as they really are but only about how a religious person perceives them to be. The believer finds an orientation in life through the sacred, perceives its manifestations through faith, understands its meanings through beliefs and lives near to it in religious practice. To speak of the ineffable mystery behind all things as an assumption of the religious person makes no comment at all about the existence of such a mystery but it says something quite fundamental about the meaning of religion itself.

The phenomenologist therefore maintains *epochē*, suspending judgements about what causes the manifestations perceived by religious faith. His task is not to affirm or deny what lies behind the hierophanies but to use the phenomenological method to describe them as they are interpreted through beliefs and expressed in religious life and practice.

Summary

In this chapter, I have offered revisions to some of the principal components in the phenomonological study of religion by distinguishing between the sacred and its manifestations which believers perceive through faith and comprehend through beliefs as tangible indicators of their unrestricted value. Following Eliade, I have also posited that the sacred defines for the religious consciousness a universal way of viewing and apprehending reality. These refinements have been necessary for us to achieve the final steps in the phenomenological method which we address in the concluding chapter by explaining and exemplifying the eidetic intuition.

References

Cox, J. L.   1980   'The influence of A. G. Hogg over D. G. Moses: A missionary message for India', *Religion and Society*, XXVII, 66–79.

Eliade, M.   1959   *The Sacred and the Profane*, trans. W. R. Trask (New York, Harcourt, Brace).

Eliade, M.   1969   *The Quest: History and Meaning in Religion* (Chicago, Univ. of Chicago Press).

Hughes, E. R.   1954   *Chinese Philosophy in Classical Times* (London, Dent).

Moses, D. G.   1939   'The problem of truth in religion', in International Missionary Council, *The Authority of the Faith* (London, Oxford Univ. Press, Madras Series Vol. 1), 63–89.

Moses, D. G.   1954   'Christianity and the non-Christian religions', *International Review of Missions*, XLIII, 146–54.

Smart, N.   1973   *The Phenomenon of Religion* (New York, Seabury).

Smith, W. C.   1978   *The Meaning and End of Religion* (San Francisco, Harper and Row).

Questions and Activities

Questions for discussion

1. What is meant by calling faith 'an organ of perception'? How does this help distinguish faith from beliefs?
2. Define the sacred in your own words. Discuss your definition in the light of the idea that the words cannot be equated with the sacred itself but only point towards hierophanies.
3. Distinguish the sacred from the unrestricted value using Smart's idea of the 'focus of faith'.
4. What is meant by the idea that the sacred is a category of the religious consciousness?
5. If 'God' is a symbol for an ineffable mystery, does 'God' actually exist? How would a phenomenologist attempt to answer this question?

Projects and activities

1. Draw a picture or an image of the sacred. Beneath it, write what you mean by the image. Then write a short essay (four to five pages) in which you distinguish between your pictorial and linguistic symbols and the sacred itself. Include in your discussion how your vision of the

sacred is perceived (faith), what the manifestations of the sacred are, and what beliefs you have expressed.

2. Participate in the following exercise:

Day 1: Read a section of your choice from the *Qur'ān*.
Day 2: Read a section of your choice from the *Chandogya Upanishads*.
Day 3: Read a section of your choice from the Hebrew Scriptures.
Day 4: Read a section of your choice from the Christian Scriptures.
Day 5: Read a section of your choice from the *Tao Te Ching*.

After each reading, answer the following questions:
a) Are any hierophanies present in this section?
b) If so, how are they apprehended?
c) What beliefs are expressed?
d) What is the focus of faith?

After reviewing your notes for each day, write a five-page essay expressing your observations of this exercise.

Chapter Ten
The Eidetic Intuition: Seeing into the Meaning of Religion

When we discussed the steps in the phenomenological method, we indicated that the concluding stages involve seeing into or intuiting the meaning of religion through the use of the paradigmatic model and then testing this intuition by a careful analysis of the phenomena from a believer's point of view. The paradigmatic model does not offer an explanation of the meaning of religion: it merely helps the phenomenologist achieve understanding through a study of how various traditions fill in the content at each stage of the model.

I seek in this chapter to help the student understand the final steps within the phenomenological method by presenting three examples of the eidetic intuition, one of which is my own. The first two examples are examined in terms of their positive contributions to the understanding of religion and then tested according to the phenomenological stages. In the light of this test I present my own intuition as a revision of the previous two.

J. E. Barnhart: Religion as the core concern with finitude

In the first chapter, we referred to Barnhart's helpful analysis of the problems associated with the definitions of religion. We now return to Barnhart for an example of a modern scholar's understanding of the meaning of religion.

Barnhart (1977, 7–11) concludes that all religious phenomena contain, and thus help the scholar to identify, what he calls a 'core concern'. This is a central 'preoccupation' with a problem experienced in life which every religion addresses and to which every religion responds. He finds that this core concern deals with the human condition of finitude.

Finitude implies that there is a basic limitation within many areas of human existence which impinge directly on an individual's or a people's well-being. Barnhart says that some examples of finitude to which religion offers a response include 'being overwhelmed with confusion, disorder, a sense of chaos, images of destruction, incurable boredom or a sense of overwhelming guilt, meaninglessness or ignorance' (p. 11).

These examples point towards the physical, psychological, social and what might be called the spiritual (for example, in an awareness of meaninglessness) dimensions within human life. Barnhart says the phenomena of any religion tend to 'cluster' around these dimensions. Included in the phenomena are 'rituals, words, documents, prayers, beliefs and special experiences'. Each phenomenon results from and responds to the problem of human finitude.

Barnhart argues that the failure to recognize that the 'cluster' of phenomena in response to a people's core concern has caused many misunderstandings among scholars of religion. One example he gives of this is the 'fruitless' debate over whether or not religion includes magic. Magic has generally been defined as the ways in which people seek to manipulate elements in life such as illness, death, social disorder, the need for retribution or injustice which lie beyond their control. So-called 'magical practices', therefore, 'have often developed in response to the core concern' (1977, 10).

Barnhart thus sees meaning in religion by seeking to understand what the phenomena actually achieve or accomplish for the believers. By trying to get inside the adherent's perspective, he identifies a central preoccupation with finitude within every religion. Although the actual 'clusters' within the phenomena differ in various traditions, they all address this common issue within human existence.

Martin Prozesky: Religion as the quest for ultimate well-being

Closely related to Barnhart's theory is the explanation by Martin Prozesky (1984, 161–3) of the University of Natal that religion is a 'quest for ultimate well-being'. Prozesky suggests that humans discover that 'the thing which most matters to us' is 'beyond the limits of our own minds' and hence beyond our ability to 'ensure'. This places humans in a condition of dependence on 'strange forces that surpass our comprehension and control'. Central to this explanation, Prozesky acknowledges, is the concept of 'human finitude'.

What people seek to ensure is their own well-being — defined initially by Prozesky as 'real benefits, real satisfactions, real successes in the struggle with suffering' (p. 162). The well-being sought, however, is ultimate and hence is always outside human control.

For Prozesky the term ultimate has a subjective and an objective meaning. Each religious tradition defines for itself (subjectively) what is most important for its well-being. These subjective perceptions, Prozesky says, 'are apt to change with deepening awareness'. There is also an objective meaning for the ultimate which Prozesky defines as 'that which cannot be surpassed, the final uttermost reality on which any prospect of complete or perfect well-being depends'.

The subjective perception of what constitutes a people's well-being merely 'approximates' the objective reality. But since the subjective perception never attains the objective reality, religious traditions continually persist in their quest. Prozesky explains: 'The drive to improve things will go on as the pressure for complete satisfaction relentlessly sets up and then undermines its conjectures at whatever really is ultimate' (1984, 163).

Prozesky arrives at this conclusion after thoroughly reviewing many religious traditions within what he calls a 'global perspective'. He concludes that religion is 'a seeking to diminish or overcome evil, misery or whatever else may threaten people and a conserving or increasing what they value' (p. 18). In a manner quite similar to Barnhart, Prozesky says that religion fulfils this function by 'giving believers a sense of hope, meaning or certainty, by assuring them that the grave is but the threshold of eternity, by enlightenment, fellowship and forgiveness, or by supplying an authoritative scripture in terms of which to handle life's riddles'. These represent the benefits of religion 'as judged by the believers themselves' (ibid.).

Positive results from Barnhart and Prozesky

The eidetic intuitions of Barnhart and Prozesky are quite similar. Both identify a central human concern which every religious tradition at least partly resolves and both claim that the meanings of religion that they intuit come from a careful study of religious phenomena rather than from superimposing preconceived ideas on top of the phenomena. This effort to see reality from within the perspective of religious traditions has produced three positive benefits for the understanding of religion.

It overcomes the problem of evaluating some traditions as 'world' religions and others as 'local' religions

Many academic texts on religions refer to 'world' religions as distinct from 'local' religions or what in some books are still called 'primitive', 'basic', or 'pre-literate' religions (Lewis, 1990, 313–14). In essence, what these texts mean is that some religions deal with universal themes common to all humankind whereas others are concerned primarily with regional issues. World religions, moreover, have a universal ultimate whereas local religions worship tribal deities and venerate ancestors known only within a specific community. World religions also spread beyond local boundaries and thus are not restricted to a particular people.

Usually included among world religions are Hinduism, Buddhism, Confucianism, Taoism, Shintoism, Judaism, Christianity, Islam and sometimes Baha'i and Sikh faiths. African traditional religions and other religions of indigenous peoples are regarded as local and tribal and hence as non-universal.

Clearly, these criteria for determining a universal, as opposed to a local religion, cannot withstand close analysis. Hinduism, for example, if it can be called one religion at all, cannot be separated from Indian society. How then is it universal? Or in what sense is Judaism a universal religion since it does not seek converts actively and is connected entirely to the God of the people of Israel?

This is where Barnhart and Prozesky help us. All religions, they argue, share fundamental universal concerns. The religious preoccupation of the Karanga people of south-central Zimbabwe, for example, is as much a concern with finitude and a quest for ultimate well-being as that which is found in Christianity or Buddhism. This recognition avoids a pejorative and distorting image (often explicitly stated or implied in many textbooks) that African religions represent a lower stage in human development than the so-called world religions.

It overcomes the problem of defining religion as a belief in God

Academic textbooks on world religions often include the question about certain traditions, 'Can we call this a religion at all?' Frequently this is asked of Theravada Buddhism, which in its most original state is atheistic, or of Confucianism, which places its ultimate value on a moral order for society. Only theistic religions such as Christianity, Judaism, Islam, certain forms of Hinduism and Mahayana Buddhism are included by some scholars as *indisputably* religions — seemingly because they all possess a belief about God.

Barnhart and Prozesky help us understand that religion is not primarily a concern with *God* but with finitude or well-being. God may be regarded in some religions as the one who addresses the core concern through his own infinity and thus defines the only source which can ensure well-being. Other religions find a resolution to the concern by becoming enlightened, attaining true knowledge or discerning the moral patterns necessary for the greatest benefit to society. On the Barnhart–Prozesky model, this does not make them less religious than theistic resolutions since both address the same core concern.

It avoids defining one religion in terms of another

In his book on African religions, Benjamin Ray (1976, 50) asks if African religions should be considered primarily as monotheistic, polytheistic or pantheistic. This issue emerges from studies which show that, whereas most African religions include a belief in a supreme being, the adherents direct most of their religious practices toward their immediate ancestors. Ray asks:

> Does the widespread belief in a universal creator mean that African religions are fundamentally monotheistic? Or does the more predominant everyday concern with the lesser gods and spirits mean that African religions are essentially

polytheistic? Or do African religions consist rather in a kind of pantheism, based on an underlying notion of sacred 'force' or 'power' which permeates and controls even the gods themselves?

On the Barnhart–Prozesky model, these questions distort the ability of the scholar to see the real issues which concern the African. They result from a Western, largely missionary, idea which assumes that religions are concerned predominantly with deities conceived of as one, many or all-pervasive. Barnhart and Prozesky contend, however, that religion is not so much interested in what Ray calls the 'gods' as it is with how the 'gods' relate to the quest for ultimate well-being in the light of human finitude. To miss this point is to impose one religion's resolution to the core concern on another religion and thus to define all religions in terms of that response.

Testing Barnhart and Prozesky's use of the phenomenological method

Barnhart and Prozesky provide examples of eidetic intuitions into the meaning of religion. They also demonstrate how such intuitions can claim to have been derived by performing and maintaining *epochē*, by seeing the phenomena from the perspective of the believer, and thus of deriving their theories from an empathetic interpretation of the phenomena of religious experience.

Testing their intuitions according to the phenomenological method can be done in two ways. One is to employ the scientific empirical approach which moves back into the phenomena to determine if the data actually support their conclusions. A second is to analyse their application of the method to determine if revisions need to be made to the way they achieved their intuitions. To adopt a thorough empirical review of Barnhart's, Prozesky's or any other scholar's data obviously would take us beyond the scope of this book and, in any case, largely defines the task of future phenomenological research. But since the purpose of this book has been to describe and exemplify the phenomenological method itself, we can adopt the second approach as the basis for offering a revision of the Barnhart–Prozesky interpretation of the essence of religion. We do this by posing two critical methodological questions.

Did Barnhart and Prozesky actually perform *epochē*?

As we have seen, *epochē* requires that, as far as possible, the scholar's own presuppositions (either personal or academic) be suspended to allow the phenomena to speak for themselves. This means that the phenomenologist tries to see into the phenomena from the point of view of the believer. Although Barnhart and Prozesky claim to have arrived at their meanings of religion in this way, the terms finitude and ultimate well-being are subject to the charge that they have been read into the phenomena rather than having emerged from them.

The idea that religion results from the core concern with finitude and thus represents a quest for ultimate well-being resembles closely what we described earlier as the projectionist theory of Ludwig Feuerbach. For Feuerbach humans invent divine beings out of their own needs and thus project on to them the qualities which they most want in themselves but which they possess only imperfectly. In Barnhart's analysis, humans feel powerless and thus create means of attaining power through forces greater than themselves. Prozesky contends that humans are unable to ensure their ultimate well-being and thus must turn to powers which they believe are able to do so.

As projectionist theories, Freud's reduction of religion to psychological need and Marx's definition of religion as a tool to keep the oppressed in a condition of slavery might, in certain respects, correspond with the views of Barnhart and Prozesky. Freud interpreted religion as a psychological *feeling* of powerlessness whereas Marx called it a socio-economic *condition* of powerlessness. Finitude certainly represents powerlessness and the efforts to overcome it either psychologically or sociologically fit into descriptions of the human quest for ultimate well-being.

That Barnhart and Prozesky seem to follow the projectionist approach so closely is not wrong in itself. *They might be right.* But they are not right *from a believer's perspective.* As we have noted earlier, the adherent does not see his own religious life, practice, beliefs and faith as a psychological or sociological projection. Rather, he sees his religion as symbolizing the very structure of reality itself. The fact that Barnhart and Prozesky present an intuition into the meaning of religion in a way which would sound quite alien to a believer suggests that they actually failed to perform *epochē* and thus have arrived at a distorted interpretation.

Have Barnhart and Prozesky preferred soteriological over numinological beliefs?

Barnhart and Prozesky identify religion as a response to a central human problem and hence tend to emphasize that the phenomena primarily contain soteriological beliefs from which numinological and anthropological beliefs are derived. This would mean that beliefs about the unrestricted value are determined by the core concern rather than the core concern being determined by the unrestricted value. In the chapter on beliefs, I described the relationship the other way round, giving precedence to the numinological belief as the source for the soteriological.

In Christianity, for example, I have described Jesus Christ as the ultimate hierophany and thus the focus for Christian faith. From this sacred manifestation, Christians define the nature of God and understand their own condition of sinfulness. If we follow Barnhart and Prozesky, however, it is the sense of sinfulness or alienation within the human which produced the need for a numinological belief in an incarnate saviour. In other words, the incarnate Christ (the numinological belief) originates from the Christian perception of sin (the soteriological belief).

The beliefs which are derived from the phenomena of many religious traditions seem to suggest something different from what Barnhart and Prozesky suggest when seen from the believer's perspective. In Vedantic Hinduism, for example, the numinological belief in *Brahman–Atman* makes an appeal in its own right and thus for an adherent it possesses intrinsic value. This is confirmed in the practice of meditation on the sacred sound OM. Although it helps lead a believer to salvation from ignorance, this meditation is undertaken so that the adherent may experience the joy of Pure Consciousness. The failure to achieve the bliss of Pure Consciousness defines for the Vedantist his need for salvation, but this is quite different from suggesting that a feeling of dissatisfaction has produced a means to overcome it through a belief in *Brahman–Atman*. From the believer's perspective the numinological outlines the need to which the soteriological responds.

This same relationship can be seen in Taoism. The unnamed Tao manifests itself in the names attributed to it. The Taoist, therefore, seeks to meditate on the meanings of the named Tao in order to be as near the sacred mystery as is humanly possible. He does this, not because of some existential crisis in life as Barnhart and Prozesky seem to suggest, but because to be near the Tao defines its own inherent attraction. If there is a life problem for the Taoist it is defined as moving away from the natural simplicity which being near the Tao entails.

Even in religions such as Christianity which seem to be soteriological in nature, a strong argument can be made that the believer wants to be one with God by being 'in Christ'. This condition, if it is understood in the light of the teachings of Jesus in the Gospel of John about being one with the Father, reflects a communion of the believer himself with the Father through Christ. Hence, the central numinological belief in Christianity that God is Father, Son and Spirit can be experienced by the believer as living in an eternal communion with the Father through the Son in the bond of the Spirit. This means that the numinological belief delineates for Christians, just as it does for the Vedantist and the Taoist, what the human predicament is and prescribes the means for solving it.

We can see this relationship quite clearly if we return to the Vedantic response to the human problem created by the belief in karma and the transmigration of souls. The essential Vedantist objection to these beliefs comes initially from the numinological category and then moves to a soteriological response. The Vedantist argues that by enslaving the individual to an endless chain of causes and effects, karma binds the soul to this world and thus keeps the individual eternally separated from *Brahman*. Karma and transmigration, however, also respond to human suffering by prescribing knowledge of the *Brahman–Atman* as the means of salvation. This response, however, is defined for the believer as the pure bliss of the realization itself which clearly is derived from the numinological belief.

From the above examples we see that numinological and soteriological beliefs are closely interrelated and also why Barnhart and Prozesky's explanations offer plausible explanations of the religious response. Eliade can even be interpreted in the light of soteriological beliefs if we suggest that every manifestation of the sacred 'saves' the believer from the homogeneity of space and time. But to do so is to miss the believer's perspective that living near the sacred defines what is really real and therefore attractive in its own right.

This may be a fine distinction, but it is an important one. To see religion as a means of overcoming fundamental human problems alone is to ignore that the focus of faith is paramount from a believer's perspective; it is his unrestricted value defining every other aspect of his life. Moreover, the focus represents a manifestation of the sacred which, if my analysis following Eliade is correct, represents the structure of the religious consciousness irreducible to human psychological and sociological conditions.

The distinction I am making is one which applies also in other disciplines, such as ethics, where the difference is drawn between an object's intrinsic and its extrinsic value. An ethical principle may be valued for the results it produces rather than for its own sake. If so, it possesses extrinsic value: its value lies outside itself. But if it possesses value in its own right regardless of its consequences, its value is called intrinsic. The philosopher Immanuel Kant argued, for example, that one ought to do one's moral duty regardless of the consequences to oneself or to others. Duty possesses an inherent value and is not primarily an instrument for achieving other, higher ends.

Numinological beliefs possess intrinsic value for adherents. The object of faith represents the highest and best that they know. Soteriological beliefs possess extrinsic value since they attempt to resolve a fundamental problem defined in terms of the end the believer is seeking. Barnhart and Prozesky suggest that religion is an extrinsic object in quest of the intrinsic value. This necessarily leads them to emphasize the functional nature of religion through its soteriological beliefs. Although their analysis is extremely helpful, it is on this point and its related failure to perform *epochē* that a revision of their eidetic intuitions is required.

A revised eidetic intuition

The revised eidetic intuition which follows aims at affirming the adherents' focus of faith as the most critical element towards which the phenomena point while still incorporating the positive benefits of the Barnhart–Prozesky interpretation to which I referred earlier. My suggestion for the essential meaning of religion is summarized in the following statement of the eidetic intuition: *every religion seeks to achieve and to maintain trust in the unrestricted value.*

According to this statement, trust is the critical component of religion from a believer's perspective. The word here is used both as a verb and a noun. To trust means 'to place one's confidence in' and its meaning as a verb is reflected in the phrase 'to seek to achieve'. Trust as a noun is the condition of having attained confidence, implied through the idea of maintaining that condition as an end in itself.

The idea of seeking to achieve trust is consistent with Barnhart and Prozesky's understanding of religion as a response to human problems and as a quest to attain an end. It is not, however, a projection on to the data of religious experience but results from the performance of *epochē* and hence is derived from the believer's perspective. Moreover, the understanding of trust as an end in itself enables the seeking after and the attainment of trust to be defined in terms of a tradition's unrestricted value and thus through numinological beliefs.

The intuition of trust as a result of performing *epochē*

If this version of the eidetic intuition is correct, each religion would regard the statement as being consistent with its own understanding of its particular tradition. Every believer could affirm that trust is what he is seeking or enjoying through myths, rituals, sacred practitioners, art, scripture and morality. Moreover, he could assert that the beliefs contained within these phenomena enable trust to occur through the exercise of faith and enable trust to be maintained through the interpretation of the activity of faith. We could conclude, therefore, that *epochē* had been performed.

To test if this is true, we will look at the particularly difficult example of Theravada Buddhism. This form of Buddhism is often labelled as atheistic because its unrestricted value is 'nirvana' which roughly translated means 'to extinguish'. In this case, faith points towards the extinguishing of human desires or attachments which keeps humans enslaved to a world of suffering.

The idea of trust is not evident here until one sees that for the believer nirvana is not just a psychological escape from the entrapments of human desire but an end in itself, a word for an indescribable sacred reality. To enter nirvana means the cessation of existence into something utterly indescribable and outside the experience of those who have not yet been enlightened. That is why some people see it only in a negative sense leading to annihilation. Nirvana, however, is the overcoming of every duality in life (pleasure and pain, one and the many, subject and object, love and hatred, real and unreal, etc.) and hence is incomprehensible to the unenlightened. Since the dualities perpetuate suffering, they need to be extinguished (Abe, 1974, 12-13).

The Theravada Buddhist, therefore, has confidence that the search for enlightenment actually leads somewhere (Smith, 1972, 51). Siddhartha Gautama set out on a journey to see into the very nature of reality. He accomplished his goal. The adherent's journey towards enlightenment also leads somewhere. The end of the seeking is a finding, although what precisely is found cannot be described. That requires trust.

Once attained, trust becomes an experience which the adherent enjoys and into which he seeks to lead others. The enjoyment of the experience and the methods into which others are encouraged on their own search are expressed in the phenomena. The supreme model for trust is the Buddha, who did not cease to exist after his enlightenment but remained in this world in order to lead others on to their own pathway towards enlightenment.

The Buddhist example, therefore, confirms from a believer's perspective that an act of trust occurs as the seeker sets out towards enlightenment and that an experience of trust results once the enlightenment is attained. The Buddhist example also shows how the eidetic intuition has been derived through the phenomenological steps beginning with *epochē* and moving through the phenomena towards beliefs, faith and the unrestricted value and back into beliefs and the phenomena as the unrestricted value is interpreted. Moreover, the structure of the religious consciousness is confirmed through the Buddhist's trust that an ultimately indescribable sacred reality stands behind all the phenomena and beliefs.

Trust and the types of belief

The idea of trusting suggests that the believer directs his attention toward his unrestricted value. His aim is to achieve trust in that value and to maintain it. This implies that from the believer's perspective the numinological belief determines the soteriological and the anthropological beliefs. To test this, we turn once more to the difficult example of Theravada Buddhism.

As we have learned, Siddhartha Gautama became aware of his need for enlightenment after he first learned that suffering defines the central human problem. The story relates how the young prince was shielded by his father from the harsh realities of the world. Even when he had grown up and had married, Siddhartha never ventured out of his father's palace into the world of pain. One day, however, he went outside the palace in his royal chariot. He saw first a sick person, then an old person and then a dead body being carried in a funeral procession. Each time, he asked his charioteer the meaning of these things and each time he heard the reply: 'This, master, happens to every man.' In one day, Siddhartha became aware of the fact that illness, old age and death occur eventually to every human being. He then saw a monk dressed in his robes of austerity begging for support and asked his charioteer the meaning of this person. He was told that this man had renounced the world to seek the meaning of truth.

The young prince decided to give up his claims to royalty, to leave his wife and child, to renounce all his riches and to set out on his own search for the meaning of life. After many years his search was still unsatisfied as neither Vedantic philosophy nor extreme self-denial presented any answers. He was eventually enlightened while seated under an Indian fig tree in a state of deep meditation. In this state, he saw that the cause of suffering is craving for pleasure or the avoiding of pain and that the way of release is to learn to follow the middle way between any desire for pleasure or any abhorrence of pain. He then went forth to teach others what he had discovered (Percheron, 1982, 22–31).

Although, apparently, Siddhartha was motivated to search for enlightenment in response to the critical problem of human suffering, closer analysis reveals that he had a prior idea of trust before he ever set foot out of his royal palace. He could have had a different reaction to the suffering he observed that day; he might even have adopted a hedonistic attitude in which he sought to maximize his own pleasure at the expense of others. The problem of human suffering, however, presented for him a religious difficulty.

Simply put, Siddhartha could not trust a reality which offered no resolution of the problem of suffering. He had confidence, however, that what he saw on his chariot journey did not define the actual meaning of human existence. There must be something else beyond illness, old age and death. This trust enabled him to persist through his disillusionment with Vedantic philosophy and his failure through asceticism. The pre-enlightened Siddhartha held a belief, however ill-defined, that an unrestricted value for life exists. He acted on that trust. Otherwise, he never could have become enlightened.

It is for this reason that the Buddhist example, although seeming to begin with the need for salvation, actually demonstrates how the numinological beliefs circumscribe soteriological and anthropological beliefs. This confirms our contention that, from the believer's perspective, the meaning of religion is not a functional response to a critical human problem but a trust in the unrestricted value.

Implications for religious studies

This interpretation of the eidetic intuition retains the positive benefits that we noted in the Barnhart–Prozesky examples. The act of trusting occurs within all religions and thus negates the pejorative distinction between universal and local religions. Moreover, this interpretation does not require that a religion possess a belief in God in order to be classified as a religion. The act of trusting and maintaining trust in the unrestricted value fits equally well into the Buddhist example where faith perceives the sacred manifestation as enlightenment leading towards the indescribable sacred called nirvana, as it does, for example, in African religions where the unrestricted value is generally the ability to feel at home in one's universe. Finally, this interpretation avoids the problem of defining one religion in terms of another since trust does not prescribe the content of the focus of faith but portrays a believer's relationship to it.

The eidetic intuition presented here, however, does seek to apply the phenomenological steps faithfully in order to attain understanding. This is why *epochē* forms the starting point and why it ultimately serves as a critical criterion for evaluating the credibility of any explanatory theory. Barnhart and Prozesky lapsed into functional explanations congenial to soteriological beliefs because they superimposed a projectionist theory on to the phenomena prior to attaining their eidetic intuitions.

The final test for any eidetic intuition, involves a return to the phenomena themselves and an evaluation of the methodologies used to attain the intuition. The ongoing work of religious research requires continued descriptive studies in order to test interpretive theories and to make revisions where necessary. The phenomenologist also examines the methodologies used, calling into question conclusions which explain religious phenomena in terms other than religious categories themselves. The trust explanation, therefore, must be tested both with reference to the phenomena and according to its consistency with the stages in the phenomenological method. In so far as it has been faithful to the method, it can be relied on as presenting an explanation of religion in and of itself, and in so far as it is confirmed by the phenomena, it can be regarded as a useful paradigm for understanding religion in general.

Summary

We have now reached a conclusion regarding the various components comprising the paradigmatic model for the study of any religion as the basis for attaining the eidetic intuition into the meaning of religion in general. These components have operated like building blocks and, as we have seen in the last two chapters, have undergone some revisions or modifications as new dimensions to the overall diagram have been discussed and added. I list below a final summary of the stages within the phenomenological method (see Figure 10.1).

Figure 10.1:   THE PHENOMENOLOGICAL METHOD

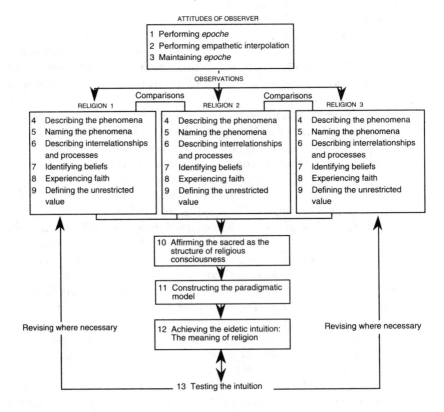

1. *Performing epochē:* The observer suspends any pre-conceived personal or academic ideas about religion or the religious tradition he proposes to observe.

2. *Performing empathetic interpolation:* The observer inserts what may be foreign, strange or alien to him into his own experience in order to attain a 'feeling for' what remains outside his experience.

3. *Maintaining epochē:* The observer suspends truth verdicts about the beliefs derived from the phenomena, the actual perception of faith, the truth of the unrestricted value or the existence of the sacred.

4. *Describing the phenomena:* The phenomenologist observes the actual practices of the adherents.

5. *Naming the phenomena:* The phenomenologist divides the phenomena into categories of the expressions of the unrestricted value in the form of myths, rituals, art, sacred practitioners, scripture and morality including general conclusions about the nature of the phenomena among many religious traditions.

6. *Describing interrelationships and processes:* The phenomenologist lists dynamic relations and developments among the classifications of the phenomena within a religion.

7. *Identifying beliefs:* The observer records thoughts, ideas or opinions about the unrestricted value and the cognitive meaning of the manifestations derived from the phenomena.

8. *Experiencing faith:* Since faith is a way for believers to perceive the unrestricted value and enables them to see and experience the sacred manifestations, the researcher includes it in his study.

9. *Defining the unrestricted value:* The phenomenologist characterizes the object or focus of faith for believers, which, although ultimate in human terms, is a hierophany capable of manifesting itself through other hierophanies.

10. *Affirming the sacred:* From a believer's point of view, the observer identifies an indefinable and unnameable mystery standing behind all religious traditions comprising the structure of religious consciousness.

11. *Constructing the paradigmatic model:* The phenomenologist constructs the pattern according to which any religion can be studied and out of which the eidetic intuition may be achieved.

12. *Achieving the eidetic intuition:* The observer 'sees into' the meaning or essence of religion in general.

13. *Testing the intuition:* The researcher goes back to the phenomena to determine the accuracy of the eidetic intuition from the point of view of the believers.

Concluding remarks

After reading this book the student should be in a position to evaluate a variety of approaches to religion in the light of the phenomenological method, to use it in his own research and further studies, and to develop his own critical observations about any theories regarding the meaning of religion.

In conclusion, the student should be reminded that this method is a discipline within religious studies and thus endeavours to understand religion in its own terms. It does not, however, restrict the study of religion to this method. Phenomenology does not claim to be the *only way* to study religion. In this regard, the student is reminded of our earlier references to Harold Turner's distinction between the phenomena and the milieu into which the phenomena are interwoven (Chapter Three) and of the inherent limitations within the method itself (Chapter Two).

The phenomenological method, however, does reserve for religious people the right to define what their religion means as expressed in the phenomena, verbalized in beliefs, apprehended in faith, and manifested through sacred intrusions into the profane world. Finally, the phenomenologist argues that it is only by adopting the perspective of adherents and experiencing their traditions from 'within' that the observer can actually attain a fair and objective view from 'without'.

References

ABE, M. 1974 'Buddhist *nirvana*: Its significance in contemporary thought and life', in S. J. Samartha (ed.), *Living Faiths and Ultimate Goals* (Maryknoll, Orbis Books), 12–22.

BARNHART, J. E. 1977 *The Study of Religion and its Meaning* (The Hague, Mouton).

LEWIS, J. R. 1990 'Images of traditional African religions in surveys of world religions', *Religion*, XX, 311–22.

PERCHERON, M. 1982 *Buddha and Buddhism* (Woodstock NY, Overlook Press).

PROZESKY, M. 1984 *Religion and Ultimate Well-being* (London, Macmillan).

RAY, B. C. 1976 *African Religions* (Englewood Cliffs, Prentice-Hall).

SMITH, W. C. 1972 *The Faith of Other Men* (San Francisco, Harper and Row).

Questions and Activities

Questions for discussion

1. Discuss and compare the meaning of the following sets of terms: a) 'core concern' and 'quest for'; and b) 'finitude' and 'ultimate well-being'.
2. Why is it a distortion to exclude African traditional religions from the category of 'world religions'?
3. How do Prozesky and Barnhart achieve an inclusive intuition by refusing to restrict the meaning of religion to a belief in God?
4. List and then discuss the objections presented in this chapter to the Barnhart–Prozesky eidetic intuition.
5. Critically evaluate the author's intuition that religion is 'trust in the unrestricted value'.
6. Define the phenomenological test for the eidetic intuition.

Projects and activities

1. Write your own explanation of the eidetic intuition and then test it within one religious tradition. Indicate in what ways the test confirms your intuition or calls for modifications.
2. Draw three diagrams or charts which depict your understanding of Barnhart's, Prozesky's and Cox's interpretations of the eidetic intuition. Write one page on each diagram explaining its meaning.
3. Make a list of what you conceive to be the strengths of the phenomenological method in the study of religion. Then make a list summarizing what you think are its weaknesses. Write an essay stating your evaluation of the method using your lists.

Bibliography and suggestions for further reading

ABE, M. 1974 'Buddhist *nirvana*: Its significance in contemporary thought and life', in S. J. Samartha (ed.), *Living Faiths and Ultimate Goals* (Maryknoll, Orbis), 12–22.

ALI, A. Y. (trans. and commentator) 1977 *The Glorious Qur'ān* (n.p., Muslim Students' Association of the United States and Canada).

ALLEGRO, J. 1977 *Lost Gods* (London, Joseph).

ALLEN, D. 1985 *Philosophy for Understanding Theology* (London, SCM Press).

ALLEN, D. 1978 *Structure and Creativity in Religion: Hermeneutics in Mircea Eliade's Phenomenology and New Directions* (The Hague, Mouton).

AYER, A. J. 1982 *Philosophy in the Twentieth Century* (London, Heidenfield and Nicolson).

BARNHART, J. E. 1977 *The Study of Religion and Its Meaning* (The Hague, Mouton).

BERGER, P. L. 1969 *A Rumour of Angels* (London, Penguin).

BETTIS, J. D. 1969 *Phenomenology of Religion* (New York, Harper and Row).

BLEEKER, C. J. 1963 *The Sacred Bridge: Researches into the Nature and Structure of Religion* (Leiden, Brill).

BLEEKER, C. J. 1971 'Comparing the religio-historical and the theological method', *Numen*, XVIII, 9–29.

BLYTHIN, I. 1986 *Religion and Methodology: Past and Present* (Swansea, Ty John Penry).

BOUQUET, A. C. 1954 *Sacred Books of the World* (Harmondsworth, Penguin).

BOURDILLON, M. F..C. 1987 *The Shona Peoples* (Gweru, Mambo Press, 3rd edn.).

BOURDILLON, M. F. C. 1990 *Religion and Society: A Text for Africa* (Gweru, Mambo Press).

BRÉHIER, E. 1969 *Contemporary Philosophy — since 1850*, trans. W. Baskin (Chicago and London, University of Chicago Press).

CARMEN, J. B. 1965 'The theology of a phenomenologist', *Harvard Divinity Bulletin*, XXIX, 13–42.

CAMPBELL, J. 1982 *The Masks of God: Primitive Mythology* (Harmondsworth, Penguin).

CHIDESTER, D. 1985 'Theory and theology in the study of religion', *Religion in Southern Africa*, VI, ii, 75–94.

166

CHILDS, B. S. 1960 *Myth and Reality in the Old Testament* (Naperville IL, Allenson).

COPLESTON, F. 1965a *A History of Philosophy, Volume 7, Part I: Fichte to Hegel* (Garden City, New York, Image Books).

COPLESTON, F. 1965b *A History of Philosophy, Volume 7, Part II: Schopenhauer to Nietzsche* (Garden City, New York, Image Books).

COPLESTON, F. 1982 *Religion and the One* (New York, Crossroad Publications).

COWARD, H. 1988 *Sacred Word and Sacred Text* (Maryknoll, Orbis).

COX, J. L. 1980 'The influence of A. G. Hogg over D. G. Moses: A missionary message for India', *Religion and Society*, XXVII, 66–79.

COX, J. L. 1989 'Karma and redemption: A religious approach to family violence', *Journal of Religion and Health*, XXVIII, 16–25.

COX, J. L. 1991 *The Impact of Christian Missions on Indigenous Cultures* (Lewiston NY, Mellen).

COX, J. L. 1994 'Religious studies by the religious: A discussion of the relationship between theology and the science of religion', *Journal for the Study of Religion*, VII (2), 3–31.

CUNNINGHAM, L. *et al.* 1991 *The Sacred Quest: An Invitation to the Study of Religion* (New York, Macmillan).

DA SILVA, A. B. 1982 *The Phenomenology of Religion as a Philosophical Problem* (Gleerip, CWK).

DAVIES, J. G. 1959 'Christianity: The early Church', in R. G. Zaehner, *Concise Encyclopaedia of Living Faiths* (Boston, Beacon), 51–85.

DHAVAMONY, M. 1973 *Phenomenology of Religion* (Rome, Gregorian Univ. Press).

DURKHEIM, E. [1915] 1976 *The Elementary Forms of Religious Life*, trans. J. W. Swain (London, Allen and Unwin).

ELIADE, M. 1959 *The Sacred and the Profane*, trans. W. R. Trask (New York, Harcourt, Brace).

ELIADE, M. 1964 *Shamanism: Archaic Techniques of Ecstasy* trans. W. R. Trask (London, Routledge).

ELIADE, M. 1969 *The Quest: History and Meaning in Religion* (Chicago, Univ. of Chicago Press).

ELIADE, M. 1976 *Myths, Dreams and Mysteries*, trans. P. Mairet (London, Collins).

ELIADE, M. 1977 *From Primitives to Zen: A Thematic Sourcebook of the History of Religions* (San Francisco, Harper and Row).

ELIADE, M. and KITAGAWA, J. (eds.)   1959   *The History of Religions: Essays in Methodology* (Chicago, Univ. of Chicago Press).

FABER, F. W.   1983   'There's a wideness in God's mercy', in *Hymns and Psalms: A Methodist and Ecumenical Hymn Book* (London, Methodist Publishing House).

FERGUSON, J.   1978   *Religions of the World* (Guildford, Lutterworth).

FEUERBACH, L.   [1854] 1975   'Religion as a projection of human nature', in A. Frazier (ed.), *Issues in Religion: A Book of Readings* (New York, Van Nostrand), 115–28.

FIRTH, R.   1973   *Symbols: Public and Private* (Ithaca, Cornell Univ. Press).

FRAZER, J. G.   1923   *The Golden Bough: A Study in Magic and Religion* (London, Macmillan).

FREUD, S.   [1913]   1945 *Totem and Taboo: Resemblances between the Psychic Lives of Savages and Neurotics*, trans. A. A. Brill (New York, Vintage Books).

FREUD, S.   1961   'The future of an illusion', in *The Standard Edition of the Complete Psychological Works of Sigmund Freud: Volume XXI (1927–1931)*, trans. J. Strachey (London, Hogarth), 5–56.

FREUD, S.   1964   'The question of a *weltanschauung*', in *The Standard Edition of the Complete Psychological Works of Sigmund Freud: Volume XXII (1932–1936)*, trans. J. Strachey (London, Hogarth), 158–86.

GOMBRICH, R.   1988   *Theravada Buddhism* (London, Routledge).

GRAHAM, A. C.   1959   'Confucianism', in R. C. Zaehner, *Concise Encyclopaedia of Living Faiths* (Boston, Beacon), 365–84.

HALL, T. W., PILGRIM, R. B. and CAVANAGH, R. R.   1986   *Religion: An Introduction* (San Francisco, Harper and Row).

HEGEL, G. W. F.   [1807] 1977 *Phenomenology of Spirit*, trans. A. V. Miller (Oxford, Oxford University Press).

HEIDEGGER, M. [1975] 1982 *The Basic Problems of Phenomenology*, trans. A. Hofstadter (Bloomington, Indiana University Press).

HICK, J.   1977   'Jesus and the world religions', in J. Hick (ed.), *The Myth of God Incarnate* (London, SCM Press), 167–85.

HINNELLS, J. R. and SHARPE, E. J. (eds.)   1972   *Hinduism* (Newcastle upon Tyne, Oriel Press).

HIRSCHBERGER, J.   1976   *A Short History of Western Philosophy* (Guildford, Lutterworth).

HODZA, A. C. (comp.) and Fortune, G. (ed.)   1975   *Shona Registers Volume I* (Harare, Univ. of Zimbabwe, Dept. of African Languages).

HÖFFDING, H. [1990] 1950 *A History of Modern Philosophy*, trans. B. E. Meyer (New York, The Humanities Press).

HONKO, L. (ed.)   1979   *Science of Religion: Studies in Methodology* (The

Hague, Mouton).

HOPFE, L.   1991   *Religions of the World* (New York, Macmillan, 5th edn.).

HUGHES, E. R.   1954   *Chinese Philosophy in Classical Times* (London, Dent).

Husserl, E. 1965 'Philosophy as a rigorous science', trans Q. Lauer, in Husserl, E. *Phenomenology and the Crisis of Philosophy* (New York, Harper and Row).

HUSSERL, E.   [1913] 1978   *Formal and Transcendental Logic*, trans. D. Cairns (The Hague, Martinus Nijhoff).

HUTCHISON, J. A.   1969   *Paths of Faith* (New York, McGraw-Hill).

JOSHI, L. M.   1975   'The caste system in India', in G. S. Talib (ed.), *The Origin and Development of Religion* (Patiala, Punjab Univ.), 64–77.

KAMM, A.   1976   *The Story of Islam* (Cambridge, Dinosaur Publications).

KILEFF, C. and KILEFF, P. (eds.)   1988   *Shona Customs* (Gweru, Mambo Press).

KING, U.   1983   'Historical and phenomenological approaches to the study of religion: Some major developments and issues under debate since 1950', in F. Whaling (ed.), *Contemporary Approaches to the Study of Religion: Volume I: The Humanities* (Berlin, Mouton), 29–164.

KLOSTERMAIER, K. K.   1989   *A Survey of Hinduism* (Albany, State Univ. of New York).

KRAMER, K.   1986   *World Scriptures: An Introduction to Comparative Religion* (New York, Paulist Press).

KRIEGER, D. J.   1991   *The New Universalism: Foundations for a Global Theology* (Maryknoll, Orbis).

KRISTENSEN, W. B.   1969   'The meaning of religion', in J. D. Bettis (ed.), *Phenomenology of Religion* (New York, Harper and Row), 31–51.

KÜNG, H.   1981   *Does God Exist?*, trans. E. Quinn (New York, Vintage Books).

LARSON, G. J.   1978   'Prolegomenon to a theory of religion', *Journal of the American Academy of Religion*, XLVI, 443–63.

LESSA, W. and VOGT, E.   1965   *Reader in Comparative Religion: An Anthropological Approach* (New York, Harper and Row).

LEWIS, J. R.   1990   'Images of traditional African religions in surveys of world religions', *Religion*, XX, 311–22.

LONG, C.   1986   *Significations: Signs, Symbols and Images in the Interpretation of Religion* (Philadelphia, Fortress).

LOTT, E.   1980   *Vedantic Approaches to God* (London, Macmillan).

MCKENZIE, P. R.   1990   'Phenomenology and "The Centre": The Leicester years', in A. F. Walls and W. R. Shenk (eds.), *Exploring New Religious Movements* (Elkhart IN, Mission Focus Publications), 29–33.

MAXWELL, P.   1986   'Some reflections on the so-called phenomenological method in the study of religion', *Religion in Southern Africa*, VII, ii, 15–25.

MERLEAU-PONTY, M. 1969 'What is phenomenology of religion?', in J. D. Bettis (ed.), *Phenomenology of Religion* (New York, Harper and Row), 5–30.

MERLEAU-PONTY, M. 1986 *Phenomenology of Perception*, trans. C. Smith (London, Routledge).

MOSES, D. G. 1939 'The problem of truth in religion', in International Missionary Council, *The Authority of the Faith* (London, Oxford Univ. Press, Madras Series Vol. 1), 63–89.

MOSES, D. G. 1954 'Christianity and the non-Christian religions', *International Review of Missions*, XLIII, 146–54.

NELSON, E. W. 1935a 'Dr. Nelson's description of Eskimo customs', in H. D. Anderson and W. C. Eells, *Alaskan Natives* (Stanford, Stanford Univ. Press), 450–5.

NELSON, E. W. 1935b 'Nelson's description of Eskimo folk tales', in H. D. Anderson and W. C. Eells, *Alaskan Natives* (Stanford, Stanford Univ. Press), 455–64.

NOSS, D. S. and NOSS, J. B. 1990 *A History of the World's Religions* (New York, Macmillan, 8th edn.).

OQUILLUK, W. A. 1981 *People of Kawerak* (Anchorage, Alaska Pacific Univ. Press).

OSWALT, W. H. 1967 *Alaskan Eskimos* (San Francisco, Chandler).

PANIKKAR, R. 1981 *The Unknown Christ of Hinduism* (Maryknoll, Orbis).

PARRINDER, E. G. 1981 *African Traditional Religion* (London, Sheldon Press).

PERCHERON, M. 1982 *Buddha and Buddhism* (Woodstock NY, Overlook Press).

PETTERSSON, O. and AKERBERG, H. 1981 *Interpreting Religious Phenomena* (Stockholm, Almquist and Wiksell).

PHILLIPS, D. Z. 1976 *Religion without Explanation* (Oxford, Blackwell).

PLANTINGA, R. J. 1989 'W. B. Kristensen and the study of religion', *Numen*, XXXVI, 173–88.

PLATVOET, J. G. 1990 *Akan Traditional Religion. A Reader* (Harare, Univ. of Zimbabwe, Dept. of Religious Studies, Classics and Philosophy).

PLATVOET, J. G. 1982 *Comparing Religions: A Limitative Approach* (The Hague, Mouton).

PREUS, J. S. 1987 *Explaining Religion: Criticism and Theory from Bodin to Freud* (New Haven, Yale Univ. Press).

PREUS, J. S. 1989 'Explaining religion: Author's response', *Religion*, XIX, 324–9.

PROZESKY, M. 1984 *Religion and Ultimate Well-being* (London, Macmillan).

PROZESKY, M.   1985   'Is there a place in Religious Studies for the criticism and re-formulation of religion', *Religion in Southern Africa*, VI, i, 71–90.

PYE, M.   1979   *The Buddha* (London, Duckworth).

RADHAKRISHNAN, S. (trans. and commentator)   1974   *The Principal Upanishads* (London, George Allen and Unwin).

RAY, B. C.   1976   *African Religions* (Englewood Cliffs, Prentice-Hall).

RINGGREN, H. (ed.)   1976   *Faculty of Theology at Uppsala University* (Stockholm, Almquist and Wiksell).

RUDOLPH, K.   1989   'Mircea Eliade and the "history" of religions', *Religion*, XIX, 101–27.

SAMKANGE, S.   1968   *Origins of Rhodesia* (London, Heinemann).

SCHMID, G.   1979   *Principles of an Integral Science of Religion*, trans. J. Wilson (The Hague, Mouton).

SEGAL, R. 1983 'In defense of reductionism', *Journal of the American Academy of Religion*, 51 (1), 97–124.

SEGAL, R.   1989   'Religionist and social scientific strategies', *Religion*, XIX, 310–16.

SHARPE, E.   1971   *Fifty Key Words: Comparative Religion* (Richmond VA, John Knox Press).

SHARPE, E.   1983   *Understanding Religion* (London, Duckworth).

SHARPE, E.   1986   *Comparative Religion: A History* (London, Duckworth).

SIVARAMAN, K.   1974   'The meaning of *moksha* in contemporary Hindu thought and life', in S. J. Samartha (ed.), *Living Faiths and Ultimate Goals* (Maryknoll, Orbis), 2–11.

SMART, N.   1973   *The Phenomenon of Religion* (New York, Seabury).

SMART, N.   1983   'The scientific study of religion in its plurality', in F. Whaling (ed.), *Contemporary Approaches to the Study of Religion. Volume I: The Humanities* (Berlin, Mouton), 365–78.

SMART, N.   1984   *The Religious Experience of Mankind* (Glasgow, Collins).

SMART, N.   1986   *Concept and Empathy: Essays in the Study of Religion*, ed. D. Wiebe (London, Macmillan).

SMART, N.   1989   *The World's Religions: Old Traditions and Modern Transformations* (Cambridge, Cambridge Univ. Press).

SMITH, D. W. 1983 'Husserl's philosophy of mind', in Floistad, G. (ed.), *Contemporary Philosophy: A New Survey. Vol. 4: Philosophy of Mind* (The Hague, Martinus Nijhoff), 249–286.

SMITH, J. Z.   1982   *Imagining Religion* (Chicago, Univ. of Chicago Press).

SMITH, W. C.   1972   *The Faith of Other Men* (San Francisco, Harper and Row).

SMITH, W. C.   1978   *The Meaning and End of Religion* (San Francisco,

Harper and Row).

SMITH, W. C.   1981   *Towards a World Theology* (Philadelphia, Westminster Press).

SPIEGLBERG, H. 1982 *The Phenomenological Movement* (The Hague, Martinus Nijhoff).

STARK, R. and BAINBRIDGE, W.   1985   *The Future of Religion: Secularization, Revival and Cult Formation* (Berkeley and Los Angeles, Univ. of California Press).

STRENG, F. J.   1985   *Understanding Religious Life* (Belmont, Wadsworth).

STRENSKI, I.   1993   *Religion in Relation: Method, Application and Moral Location* (London: Macmillan).

TENRI INTERNATIONAL SYMPOSIUM 1986 *Cosmos, Life, Religion: Beyond Humanism* (Tenri, Tenri Univ. Press).

TOKAREV, S.   1989   *History of Religion* (Moscow, Progress).

TURNER, H.   1981   'The way forward in the religious study of African Primal Religions', *Journal of Religion in Africa*, XII, 1–15.

TYLOR, E. B.   1891   *Primitive Culture* (London, Murray).

TYLOR, E. B.   1965   'Animism', in W. Lessa and E. Vogt, *Reader in Comparative Religion: An anthropological Approach* (New York, Harper and Row), 10–21.

VAN DER LEEUW, G.   1938   *Religion in Essence and Manifestation* (London, Allen and Unwin).

WACH, J.   1968   *Understanding and Believing* (New York, Harper and Row).

WALLS, A. F. and SHENK, W. R. (eds.)   1990   *Exploring New Religious Movements* (Elkhart IN, Mission Focus Publications).

WHALING, Frank (ed.)   1984   *The World's Religious Traditions* (Edinburgh, Clark).

WIEBE, D.   1981   *Religion and Truth: Towards an Alternative Paradigm for the Study of Religion* (The Hague, Mouton).

WILES, M.   1977   'Myth in theology', in J. Hick (ed.), *The Myth of God Incarnate* (London, SCM Press), 148–66.

WILSON, M.   1959   *Communal Rituals of the Nyakyusa* (London, Oxford Univ. Press).

WORLD MISSIONARY CONFERENCE   1910   *Report of Commission IV: The Missionary Message in Relation to Non-Christian Religions* (Edinburgh, Oliphant, Anderson and Ferrier).

ZHUWAWO, C.   1990   'An Investigation of Vashawasha *Kurova guva* Ceremony and the Catholic Teaching on the Life after Death' (Harare, Univ. of Zimbabwe, Dept. of Religious Studies, Classics and Philosophy, BA(Hons.) dissertation).

Index